Fun with Office

Learn Coding with Visual Basic

By Bob Dukish

Website: www.dukish.com

For information: bob@dukish.com

Dukish LLC

ISBN-13: 979-8-6629-3027-8

Preface

There is a multitude of computer programming languages. Some can be cryptic and unintuitive, while others are easier to be understood by humans. The tradeoff is that friendlier and easier to use programming languages are a less efficient way to manipulate data. The most efficient way to program a computer is by directly using ones and zeros, or the next step up using hexadecimal numbers, which consolidates the job by working with the ones and zeros in groups of four. This type of programming can also use mnemonic instructions to move data throughout the hardware and perform calculations. It is called assembly programming and is very compact and powerful but difficult to grasp. Another drawback of assembly language is that it must be adapted to the computer hardware and processors involved.

We consider the machine to be at a low-level, and humans at a high-level. This text will show you how to write program code using a very easy-to-understand, high-level programming language called *Visual Basic.* If you have Office programs for word processing or spreadsheets on your computer, you have an embedded version of Visual Basic called a Visual Basic Application (VBA). The reason for its incorporation within the Office suite is to allow for greater functionality of the Office programs, but this text uses VBA as a convenient way to learn about computer programming in a fun way.

Acknowledgments

I would like to thank my students. Many of the programs presented in this text were developed with student involvement as class projects.

Code Downloads

Links to the free code downloads are available from the following Website:

www.dukish.com

The text may be copied and pasted into the IDE to save you from manually typing; however, you must take care to observe the same naming conventions outlined in the book. If there are name mismatches at the top of the control properties window, the program will not operate correctly.

When manually inputting code, it is essential that comment lines begin with an apostrophe and do not carry over to a second line. It is unnecessary to enter comment lines when typing code from the book.

About the author

Bob Dukish has spent over 40 years working and teaching in the field of technology. After serving in the military, working as an electronics component engineer, and running a corporation, Bob taught engineering at both the high school and college levels. He has Associate Degrees in Avionic Systems and Electronic Engineering Technology, a Bachelor's Degree in Physics from Syracuse University, and Master's Degrees from Rensselaer Polytechnic Institute and Kent State University, where he now teaches digital electronics and computer architecture courses.

Table of contents

Chapter 10: Custom Games

Chapter 11: Unfinished Business

Chapter one

Background on Computers and Programming

Section 1.1. The Beginning of Time

The overarching question I pose in this first section is, "Did time began with a Big Bang or just a faint tick?". Suppose I started a class session posing such a question. In that case, I'm sure a student would ask a follow-up question like, "Professor, did you skip your medications today?" I only pose the question because I like using the word "overarching". But also to pose a more pertinent question, "What came first, the computer or the program?". The term "algorithm" is another word I love. It means finding a solution to a problem through some type of structured process. Computer programming involves using algorithms, but so does living as a plant or animal on this planet. Lifeforms have developed survival algorithms over the millennia, and we humans have also developed algorithms that allow us not only to survive but to thrive.

I was first introduced to computer programming after joining the U.S. Air Force, where I worked as an electronics technician. It was a college course in Fortran programming, which I found challenging to understand and made me happy to work on the hardware end of things. In that class, a few of the computer science majors were joking about other languages. One was called APL, and the joke was that it stood for "Another Programming Language." (It actually stands for "A Programming Language.") APL, much like Fortran and the others at the time, were difficult for the novice to learn and best suited for math and scientific calculations. Fortran was developed in the 1950s and APL in the 1960s. During that time, programs ran on large mainframe computers housed in air-conditioned rooms. The users were periodically connected to the mainframe through a system of terminals and briefly allotted a tiny section of access time through a process called polling.

Although I disliked the complexity of Fortran, it was the precursor to the Basic programming language developed in the 1960s, which was designed to be more accommodating to non-scientists and people with limited mathematical ability. Microsoft popularized a version of Basic in the 1970s as home computer systems began to emerge, and it was made available in the early operating systems with the advent of the personal computer in 1981. Fortran is still in used in scientific applications. Many other nearly fifty-year-old programming languages are still in use to this day. Other thought to be extinct languages like COBOL, Pascal, and Ada (a spin-off of Pascal), are used in critical areas by government and banks. Part of the slow response to provide the first economic stimulus and unemployment payments during the Covid-19 pandemic was due, in part, to the lack of availability of programmers familiar with these legacy languages.

The electronic computer era's actual beginnings began during the Second World War when the British constructed a giant mainframe computer named Colossus. Its purpose was to break the German communication code called *Enigma*. The Enigma code was thought at the time to be unbreakable, and the German forces communicated with impunity, believing the information was secure. After the British managed to program Colossus to break the code, the Allied Forces only acted on major events, to not tip off the fact that the code had been broken and that Axis communications were being intercepted. The American version of Colossus was called ENIAC, shown in figure 1.1.

Figure 1.1

The earliest electronic computers were as big as a house. The ENIAC used over 17 thousand vacuum tubes and consumed enough power to equal a large city neighborhood's power usage. The term "electronic" is explicitly used since there were computers before the advent of electronics. The first being the abacus developed in Babylonia in around 2400 BC. The abacus made calculations more manageable. In the early 1800s, mathematician Ada Lovelace is considered the first computer programmer and wrote code for Charles Babbage's mechanical Analytical Engine. Now we have a bit more insight into the chicken vs. egg dilemma.

Section 1.2. Digital Signals

In the last section, we referred to an electronic computer and differentiated it from one that is mechanical. A more accurate description of a modern computer would be to call it a *digital* electronic computer. Along with the abacus, other versions of analog computers were used throughout history, including versions that used electricity. The difference between a digital and analog signal is that, with time represented horizontally on the x-axis and voltage represented on the y-axis, digital signals, as shown in figure 1.2, have only one of two possible voltage levels.

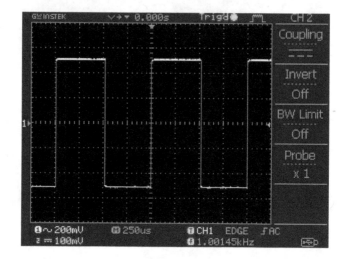

Figure 1.2

In contrast, an analog signal, shown in figure 1.3, has a continually changing voltage level with respect to time.

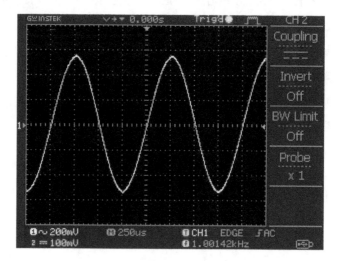

Figure 1.3

The signals shown in the figures were observed on an Oscilloscope, a versatile piece of test equipment that displays voltage waveforms. Newer style O' scopes display much of the information by calculating it automatically and showing it directly on the screen. Also, screenshots can be saved as a computer picture file or sent to a printer. With older model scopes, the user would have to reference the overlapping grid to the setting adjustments of both horizontal and vertical controls. The signal values can then be manually calculated.

The reason analog computers were abandoned back in the 1960s in favor of digital versions is that analog signals are more complex than simple, high or low, digital voltage levels. Also, analog signal levels are less tolerant of noise. (When we speak of noise in electronic applications, we are referring to electromagnetic interference.) Digital circuitry is also much easier to construct and to miniaturize. Digital computer circuits can essentially be thought of as switches that process data by turning either on, or turning off. The on condition is considered a one (high), and the off state is *zero* (low). Digital logic functions can be explained using the concepts of electricity connected to wires and switches. Figure 1.4 is an example of the AND logic function, where an open switch (as shown) is off, and represented by zero (low), and a closed switch, making contact, is represented by a one (high).

Figure 1.4

Although not shown in our diagram, the functionality is that if a source of power were located to the left of the switches with a lamp connected to the right, the first switch AND the second switch of figure 1.4 would both need to be on for the current to flow through the wire to light the lamp. Alternately the OR function is shown in figure 1.5:

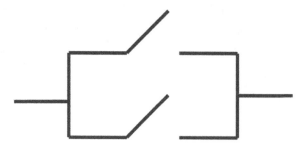

Figure 1.5

With this circuit, the situation is that either one, OR the other, switch needs to be on to allow for current flow. Both of the electric circuits presented in our figures for AND and OR logic have only two switches, but you can add additional switches to the patterns and keep the functions intact. As we move through coding examples, you will see conditional statements that utilize both the AND and OR states. Along with the AND and OR functions, we use the NOT function quite a bit. One nice feature of Visual Basic is that we simply type the words to use the conditional functions. In contrast to other programming languages, where symbols are used instead of words that tend to muck up the water for a person's first view into the process of coding.

Section 1.3. Introduction to Visual Basic

Visual Basic essentially is a program that makes programs. In its standalone version, you can make complete programs which you can distribute, and where it can have the look and feel of a typical computer program. With VB, you can open and save files, use databases, and do relatively complex operations. Many people preferred to use the standalone VB6 program, but it has now been replaced by VB.Net, which, as the name suggests, is better suited for Internet applications. This text allows you to learn to program without any need to purchase or download special programming software, provided that you have access to Microsoft Office programs like Word® or Excel®. If you are on a networked computer at work or school, you may need to change security settings to enable macros. A macro is a helper application to a program that allows for ease of operation by automating some tasks by running background code. A risk with running a macro is that hackers sometimes use them for nefarious purposes. It is never a good idea to open any unknown executable files, including Visual Basic Scripts (.vbs), since they can have dire consequences. A widespread trick a hacker will use is to gain control of a computer and then use a person's contact book to send out emails with a message telling them to open an enticing file. The result is that the file does bad things and spreads from contact to contact. Another tactic is to generate a popup with code that executes when the user clicks the *OK* button or even clicks on the *X* at the top of the window. It is best to close questionable pop-ups using the Windows task manager. As with any powerful and useful technology, bad people can misuse it and cause problems.

Visual Basic and Visual Basic Applications are object-oriented and event-driven, giving more of a free-flow, as the user has a great deal of control over the program operation. In contrast, a procedural language runs in a predetermined order where the line-after-line of code execution may occasionally jump to different areas depending on circumstances. Early languages like FORTRAN and C are procedural to the extent that when data is needed to be input, the user may be prompted. All computer programming needs to have some procedural aspects, and VB and VBA code are procedural mainly when responding to the methods of its control objects within subroutines. Code execution tends to be compartmentalized and referred to as encapsulation. Subroutine functions can be written and called as needed to supplement control object operation to make the program more procedural, robust, and useful.

Chapter One Summary

Computational machines have been around for a very long time; however, electronic computers were only developed around the middle of the last century. The first electronic computers were as big as a house and consumed the same amount of power as a large neighborhood. Transistors, and their miniaturization, led to desktop-sized computers and eventually to popular devices such as smartphones and other convenient electronic devices. Miniaturization is also due to digital electronics, which only requires switching signals between two distinct logic levels. In contrast, analog signals have an infinite range of possibilities and use much more complicated electronic circuitry. The program code for computers and other devices uses logic functions such as AND, OR, and NOT. There are many programming languages, with Visual Basic being a very natural computer language for humans to understand. It is considered an object-oriented event-driven language. We with be working with a version of that language incorporated in standard office programs and is called a Visual Basic Application. In the next chapter, we will look at getting started in different Office versions and navigate the VBA home screen.

Chapter two

Starting a Visual Basic Application

Section 2.1. Introduction to the Editor Screen

Before we get into writing code, we have to find out how to get to the Office program's macro and VB portion. Since the versions will have slightly different layouts, it may take a little experimentation to find how to get to the section where you can start writing code. It should be possible to get into Visual Basic after starting a new blank Word document by using the shortcut, Alt + F11, or possibly Fn + Alt + F11. (On a Mac Fn + Shift + F11.) If that doesn't work, we will present a few screenshots to help explain how to start Visual Basic without the shortcut. Still, suppose you are using different versions of the programs. In that case, some trial and error or research on the Internet may be needed to add the *Developer Tab* to the program ribbon (menu bar) for your specific version of Office programs. We will first demonstrate getting started by using an older version of Office with Word 2007 as the first example.

Section 2.2. Finding Visual Basic in Word 2007.

For older Office programs like Word 2007, we first click the Program button at the top left of the screen as shown in Figure 2.1, and then at the bottom of the box that appears, click the Word Options button.

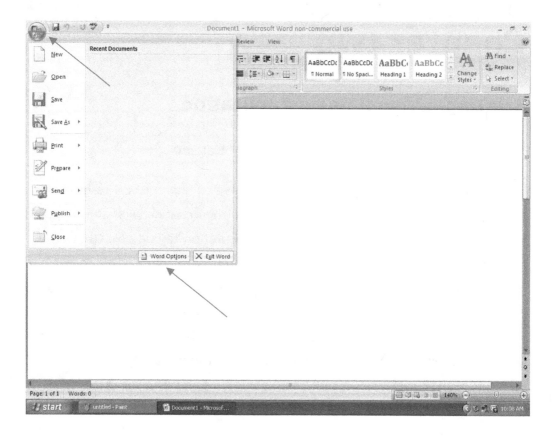

Figure 2.1

Next, as outlined in Figure 2.2, you then check the box for the *Show Developer tab in the ribbon* from the Popular Word Options selection at the top left of the screen. The ribbon is sometimes also commonly referred to as the menu bar.

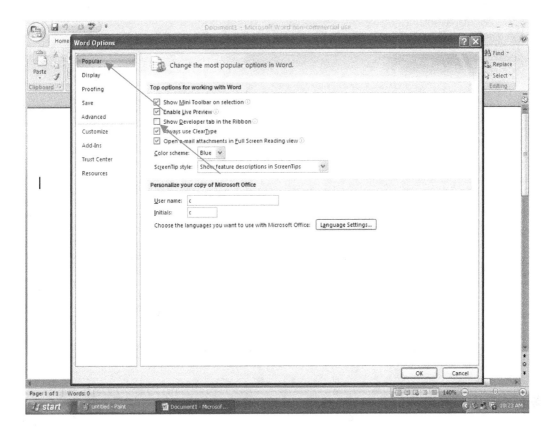

Figure 2.2

After selecting OK at the bottom of the window, the Developer Tab appears on the top menu bar. It will now appear in the menu whenever the Word or Excel programs are first opened. As shown next in Figure 2.3, after clicking the Developer Tab in the menu, you will see the Visual Basic icon appearing on the left side of the code selections. Clicking the VB icon will open the code development window where you can begin programming.

Figure 2.3

Section 2.3. Finding Visual Basic in Word 2016.

In newer versions of Office, including Office 365, the process is relatively similar. For Word 2016, as shown in Figure 2.4, we select *Options* from the left menu bar after starting a new blank document.

20

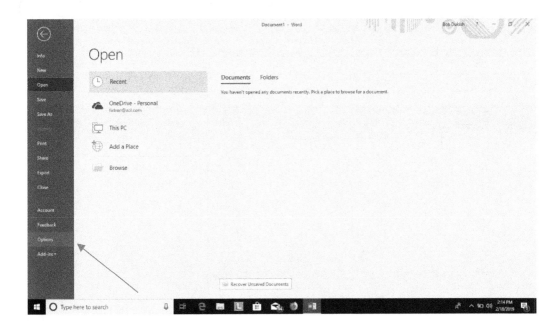

Figure 2.4

As shown in Figure 2.5, select Customize Ribbon from the left menu.

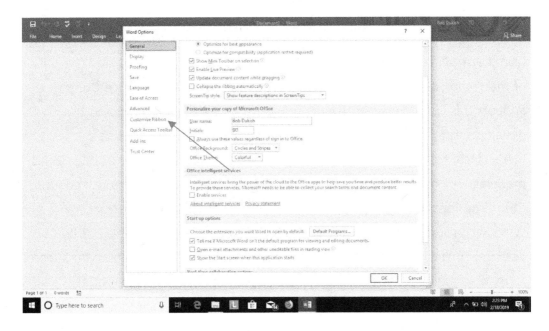

Figure 2.5

Next, check the developer box, as shown in Figure 2.6. Once you click the developer box and press OK, you will find the Visual Basic selection, as shown in the picture for Word 2007 in the previous section (Figure 2.3).

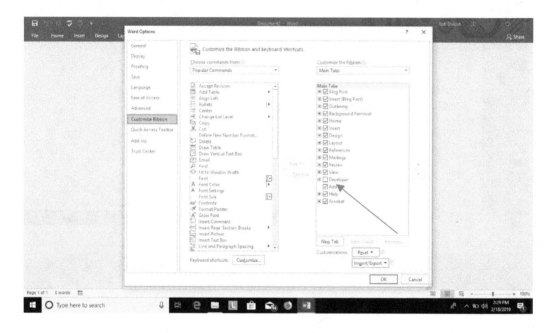

Figure 2.6

If all else fails, you can start a macro and enter the Visual Basic editor from there. Limited student versions of Office 365 may not provide the option of macros or VBA programming, but the regular version of Office 365 does support this. It is only a matter of going to the settings and adding the developer tab. Once we start the developer editor, you will notice a hierarchical tree containing areas for modules. A project can include several modules. For our purpose, we are only interested in seeing how to code a form. The form is where the user will see all of the familiar parts of a Windows program. We demonstrate how to add a form in Figure 2.7 by selecting *Insert* and then *Userform* from the dropdown box. After you start a form, you can click the handles on the form's edge to resize it. You will also notice a toolbox that contains control objects to add to the form for the user to interact with your program. Highlighting the user form should bring up the toolbox. If the toolbox is not visible, you can select view from the menu and click to show the toolbox. You can click on a control object, move the mouse to the form area, and left click to drag out the object to the size you would like. This process takes a little practice. It would be helpful first to have the form resized larger than the default size by dragging its *handles*, since some projects require more than one control object and need more space.

Figure 2.7

Later, to insert the program code, Visual Basic treats each section of code as a subroutine. Coding in VB is about as nonprocedural of a computer language, as you will find. In other words, the program does not execute from the very beginning to the very end of the entire program, but rather it runs in sections, called *subroutines*, as the user interacts with the controls placed on the form. The code for the overall project will contain these subroutines in the order that you coded them.

Chapter Two Summary

There are slightly different ways to enter the Visual Basic Application design mode, depending on the Office program and version. The online student and restricted version of Office 365 may have limited functionality, but VBA is part of the regular version of 365. The layout is similar to what we have covered in this chapter. The main objective is to go to the options menu to add the developer tab on the menu bar in order to access the Visual Basic add-on. We are able to work in the VB environment after entering the development section of the Office program. After practicing adding and resizing control objects to the form, we will code the controls in the next chapter.

Chapter three

Making a program

Section 3.1. The "Hello World" Program

In our first project, we will code the obligatory learning example that produces the output of "Hello World." Start by selecting insert userForm shown in Figure 3.1 at the top arrow to begin designing the form. Hover over the controls in the toolbox, shown by the bottom arrow, and place a *TextBox* on the form, then pick the *Button* control and place it on the form, similar to how it appears in the Figure. If the controls toolbox is not visible, single-click the form, or you can select view from the menu and click to show the toolbox.

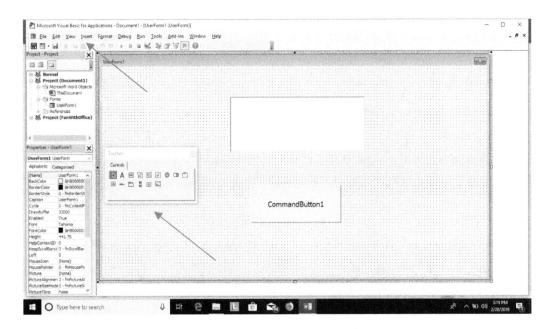

Figure 3.1

By default, the official name for the button is CommandButton1. Unless control objects are renamed, they are given the name of their function followed by an incrementing number as they are added to the form. It is good practice to rename controls immediately after placing them on the form. The standard name convention is to have three lower-case letters describing the control, which is immediately followed by a short descriptive name. (Note, there cannot be spaces in a control's name.) We will give the Command Button the name *cmdMessage* and call the Textbox *txtMessage*. There is no differentiation between upper-and lower-case text in this programming language, but sometimes capital letters can help with readability. It is good practice to name all of the controls before writing any code, or the code may not be applied correctly.

Some controls also have a *caption* property. Again, by default, the caption is given the same text as its name. In our project, it makes sense to change the caption of this button to, "Get a Message." The recommended way of doing this is to retype the new caption into the caption field of the properties box for the button, shown on the left side of Figure 3-1. There you may also wish to change font style and size. You may also select different colors for the font in the properties box. A more straightforward, but not recommended, way to change the caption is to retype the new caption over the old one. It can be done by clicking once on the button's caption and retyping it. We don't recommend this method because it is easy to make two clicks, which will take you to the code window. When you double click on the button, you create a subroutine section for coding the control's operation.

When you start coding, you will notice that the subroutine's beginning and ending lines are automatically inserted for you. For our project, add the following text in between the subroutine's opening and closing sections, as shown highlighted in Code Listing 3.1.

```
Private Sub cmdMessage_Click()
txtMessage = "Hello World"
End Sub
```

Code Listing 3.1, Hello World Program

You can click the play button to run the program after it has been coded, or select the *run* option from the menu. If the program is unavailable to run, click once on the form so that it is selected. If an error message is displayed, carefully check for spelling errors since there is no spellcheck when typing code. You will notice that the form displays a program name as it is running. *UserForm1* will be displayed by default at the top of the user form and may be changed in the form properties window. The form and any other objects will have their properties listed by clicking one time in order to highlight it. Also, clicking once on the form will bring back the controls toolbox if it has disappeared. If you inadvertently click twice and find yourself in a code section, you can return by selecting *view object* from the project explorer box or selecting the view option from the menu tabs. To stop the program, you can close by clicking "x" on the top right side of the window, similar to how most programs are closed. In our next section, we will create an exit button and add more functionality.

Section 3.2. Text Boxes for both Inputs and Outputs

In our last project, we used the text box to provide an output message. Text is called a *string* data type, but text boxes can also be used for numerical inputs and outputs. We can additionally store the input data in a variable, manipulate it, and output it directly or save it in a database. Our next project will give a personalized message output, and we'll add an exit button. We will be naming the top text box, *txtInput*, and the bottom *txtMessage*. The message button will be named cmdMessage, the clear button *cmdClear*, and the exit button will be called *cmdExit*. (It helps to name the controls exactly as we do, to reduce coding errors.) You may also notice writing on the form for the user to identify the different text boxes. They are called *labels* and are found in the control's toolbox. It may be interesting for you to vary the fonts, font sizes, foreground and background colors, but the form should be constructed somewhat similar to the one shown in Figure 3.2 for consistency with our program.

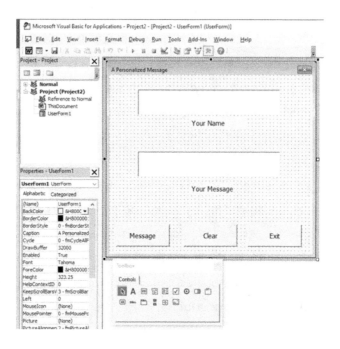

Figure 3.2. Text box input and output.

The easiest function to code is the exit button. The only code between the opening and closing lines of the subroutine is the word *End*. The subroutine listings mainly appear in the order in which they were added to the form. I added the exit button first, so its code is shown first by default. The subroutine location doesn't matter. The second easiest code to write is the clear function in which a *null string* is printed in both text boxes. Text inputs and outputs are called string information, and a null string is blank text. Null strings are coded with an open and closed set of apostrophes (""). The entire program code is presented in Code Listing 3.2.

```
Dim person As String
```
_____

```
Private Sub cmdClear_Click()
txtInput = " "         'clears both TextBoxes
txtMessage = " "
```

```
End Sub
```

```
Private Sub cmdExit_Click()
End
End Sub
```

```
Private Sub cmdMessage_Click()

If txtInput = " " Then      'gives reminder to enter name
txtMessage = "Please enter your name in the box above."
End If

If Not (txtInput = " ") Then    'since name has been entered, says hello
person = txtInput.Text
txtMessage = ("Hello " & person)
End If

End Sub
```

Code Listing 3.2. Hello Message

The output shows the word *Hello* followed by the name the person entered in the top text box. Note: Text appearing after a single apostrophe is a programmer's comment. Comment lines are used for the documentation but ignored by the program. Comments must stay on only one line, or another apostrophe would be needed. It is unnecessary to enter comment lines when typing code from the book. We highlighted our comments in Code Listing 3.2.

The last subroutine in our program does most of the work. When the message button is clicked, the code uses an, if/then conditional statement to check if the user made an entry in the top text box. If it was left blank, a message appears asking them to enter their name, and the program exits the message subroutine. We are using the NOT logic function to determine if at least one character has been input. There are three basic logic functions: AND, OR, and NOT. If the input is NOT a null string, then the string data is passed to the variable called *person*. The bottom text box will then display the word, *Hello,* and a space, followed by the string variable containing the user's name. Joining two or more strings in the output is called *concatenation*, and in this language, an ampersand is the operator used as a connector. The variable is declared to be string data in the general declarations area located at the very top of the code. It must be manually typed in, and is used by the Visual Basic program to operate on the data type correctly.

Section 3.3. Message Boxes for both inputs and outputs

Before we construct a new program, you can modify the last program to generate a MessageBox notice if the user fails to provide input information by using the previous program with the changes to cmdMessage subroutine, as shown highlighted in Code Listing 3.3.

```
Private Sub cmdMessage_Click()
If txtInput = " " Then      'gives reminder to enter name
MsgBox "Please enter your name", vbInformation, "Message Program"
End If
If Not (txtInput = " ") Then       'since name has been entered, says hello
person = txtInput.Text
txtMessage = ("Hello " & person)
End If
End Sub
```
Code Listing 3.3

The standard Windows Message Box pop up will display information to the user if they click the Message Button without entering their name. If you would like to cause the experience to be a little more stressful, replace the text in the highlighted section with the term vbExclamation or vbCritical, for a response, as shown in Figure 3.3.

Figure 3.3 Message Box Popup

Our modified project will now allow the user form to be a little less cluttered and perhaps provide a bit more intuitive operation, as shown in Figure 3.4.

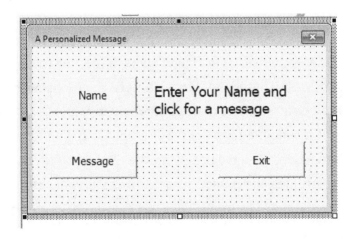

Figure 3.4. Modified Message Project

We will pop up an InputBox for the user to enter their name and run it similar to the last program. The message saying hello to the user will now occur via a MessageBox. The new code is presented in Code Listing 3.4.

```
Dim person As String
```

```
Private Sub cmdExit_Click()
End
End Sub
```

```
Private Sub cmdMessage_Click()
If person = " " Then        'gives reminder to enter name
MsgBox "Please enter your name", vbQuestion, "Message Program"

Else      'since name has been entered, says hello
MsgBox "Hello " & person, vbInformation, "Message Program"
End If
End Sub
```

```
Private Sub cmdName_Click()
person = InputBox("Enter your name", "Message Program")
End Sub
```

Code Listing 3.4 Modified Message Program

We eliminated the text boxes and replace them with popup boxes for both input and output. There is no longer a need for the clear button, and the form looks a little cleaner. Most of the action again happens in the message button section. We simplified the code by removing the conditional logic using the NOT function. Now we are using the *Else* method to display the greeting, which includes the person's name. If statements can contain multiple choices and may, as in our case, contain a final determination by using the *Else* statement as the final possibility. A subroutine will exit without performing any action when using only *If* conditions which are not satisfied, but a default outcome will occur when using the Else condition as the last case.

The program we constructed also allows the user to press *enter*, rather than clicking on the name button. It is a fairly common programming practice to *set focus* on the section of a form where the user is expected to first interact. It can be done in the code, but Visual Basic also allows the programmer to set the *tab stops* for each control. This is done by changing the tab indexes as follows: 0 for the name, 1 for the message, and 2 for the exit button. Also, the label (tab stop 4) has its *tab stop* property set to *false* so that it is bypassed when selecting buttons on the form by using the tab key.

Section 3.4. Labels as Outputs

Using the same modified form as in the last project shown in Figure 3.4, we will eliminate the message's output popup box and change the form's label to display the message. The program will operate as before except that now, the label will no longer just display a static message but will instead change as the program runs. All of the code from the last project will remain the same except for the message button subroutine, as shown in Code Listing 3.5. Only the highlighted line has been changed.

```
Private Sub cmdMessage_Click()
If person = " " Then        'gives reminder to enter name
MsgBox "Please enter your name", vbQuestion, "Message Program"

Else        'since name has been entered, says hello
Label1 = ("Hello " & person)
End If
End Sub
```

Code Listing 3.5 Changing the label

The label is called Label1 since we neglected to change its default name. The label text will change as the message button is pressed, if the user has entered a name in the InputBox.

It is also possible to create a second label leaving its properties caption field as blank, later having it display the *hello* message after the user clicks the button. The code would only need to have the second label's name substituted in the highlighted line of Code Listing 3.5.

Chapter Three Summary

Text boxes deal with letters and words. This type of data is called *string* data. (Later, we will see that through slight manipulation, text boxes can also work with numbers.) They can directly accept string data as input, as well as output string characters or string variables. We also saw that message boxes can also be used for both input and output.

It may be better to provide a label to output text in many cases rather than using either a text box or a message box. We also found the properties menu can be very helpful in designing a program to accommodate the user. VBA is not a favorite in the programming community, possibly due to its reliance on the many options of properties menus and the code's encapsulation construction utilizing subroutines. The next chapter will examine more user controls and how to load data from computer memory into the form at runtime.

Chapter Four

Bringing Image Files into a Program

Section 4.1. Displaying Pictures with User-entered Text

Using the image box from the control's toolbox, we can display a picture on a form similar to how we display user information with a label. It can be displayed continuously, or multiple images can be displayed as the user operates control objects. This program will have a text box for the user to type colors to be displayed. A select button will allow each of the following colors to be displayed: red, green, and blue. We also have a clear button to clear the image color and an exit button. The form for the project appears in Figure 4.1.

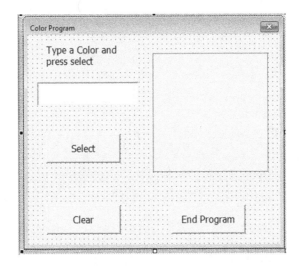

Figure 4.1 Text box input for displaying colors

The text box is named *txtInput,* and the tab index is set to 0 in the property's menu so that the mouse cursor appears at the action point when the program first starts. The *Selection* button is called *cmdSelect*, the *Clear* button is *cmdClear*, and *Exit* is *cmdExit*. We left the default name for the image, which is *Image1*. The code in the selection button section will need a path in which to locate each color. We created a new folder on the C drive and named it vb. The image box on the form was set in pixels to 150 in length by 150 in width. Using an image program such as Paint, set the picture size for the same length and width, fill the canvas with each of the four colors, and save them as bitmap files in the vb folder. We display the color white when the form is cleared, but using the same color as the form back color may look better. The code is presented in Listing 4.1.

```
Dim Color As String
```

```
Private Sub cmdClear_Click()
Image1.Picture = LoadPicture("C:\vb\white.bmp")
txtInput = ""     'clears TextBox with two ajoining quotation marks
txtInput.SetFocus 'sends cursor back to TextBox
End Sub
```

```
Private Sub cmdSelect_Click()
Color = txtInput.Text

If LCase(Color) = "red" Then
Image1.Picture = LoadPicture("C:\vb\red.bmp")

ElseIf LCase(Color) = "green" Then
Image1.Picture = LoadPicture("C:\vb\green.bmp")

ElseIf LCase(Color) = "blue" Then
Image1.Picture = LoadPicture("C:\vb\blue.bmp")

Else
MsgBox "Color Not Available", vbInformation, "Color Program"
txtInput = ""     'clears TextBox
txtInput.SetFocus 'sends cursor back to TextBox
End If
End Sub
```

```
Private Sub cmdExit_Click()
End
End Sub
```

Code Listing 4.1

The variable called *Color* is written at the top of the code in the general declaration section, where it is dimensioned as a *string* type. Strings are characters of text data. The path locates the picture on the C drive inside of the vb folder. (Don't forget to put the colon after the C:) On computers, the slash marks are slanted to the back (backslashes), unlike those used on the Internet, which uses forward-slashes to denote locations. If you would like, feel free to modify the code to display pictures. Another method of clearing the form is to replace the clearing picture with the following line of code: *Image1.visible = False*. That will make the image box disappear from the form; however, before displaying any of the colors, the line: *Image1.visible = True* would need to be added at the beginning of the *cmdSelect* subroutine code. The form can be resized to increase the size of the picture box, and more colors can be added.

The text case size matters when comparing string values since the upper and lower cases are assigned different ASCII codes to represent the letters at a more basic computer hierarchy level. In the selection code, the function LCase( ) converts whatever the user enters into lower-case letters to be matched in the *if/then, else/if* section. If a match exists, the color is displayed in the image box; otherwise, a popup message is generated telling the user the color is not available. The text box is cleared with a null string. (The set of parentheses must be directly next to each other without a space in between.) The set focus property from the properties window is set up in design mode so that after a user action, the program runs more smoothly.

Section 4.2. Displaying Pictures using Command Buttons

Each time the user clicks a button, the color choice is loaded with the white color used for clearing the picture box. Three command buttons have been added to the form and are named: *cmdRed, cmdGreen, and cmdBlue* and appear in Figure 4.2.

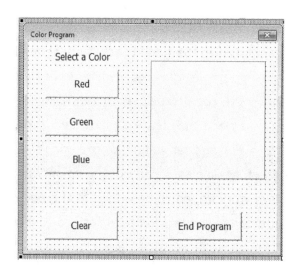

Figure 4.2 Three color selection form

The corresponding color image is loaded into the image box when the user clicks on a color. This method is more simplified than the last project. However, it would be impractical if a large number of selections were available. The Code Listing is 4.2.

```
Private Sub cmdBlue_Click()
Image1.Picture = LoadPicture("C:\vb\blue.bmp")
End Sub
```

```
Private Sub cmdClear_Click()
Image1.Picture = LoadPicture("C:\vb\white.bmp")
End Sub
```

```
Private Sub cmdGreen_Click()
```

```
Image1.Picture = LoadPicture("C:\vb\green.bmp")
End Sub


Private Sub cmdRed_Click()
Image1.Picture = LoadPicture("C:\vb\red.bmp")
End Sub


Private Sub cmdExit_Click()
End
End Sub
```

Code Listing 4.2 Three-button color program

Section 4.3. Displaying Pictures with One Button

We can clean up the form by using a single button to select from the range of colors, as pictured in Figure 4.2.

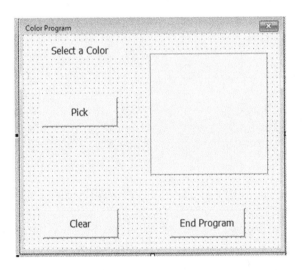

Figure 4.3 One button form

We kept the red button and deleted the buttons and code for the other selector buttons. Also, the red button's name has been changed to *cmdPick*, and by not double-clicking on the button, but by selecting view code from the menu, we changed the name at the top of the subroutine to the new button name. It is essential that the button name exactly matches the first name in the subroutine's first line. Next, we dimensioned (dim) a variable as an integer to use as a counter to keep track of the colors as described in Code Listing 4.3.

```
'this is an example of nested if - else conditions
Dim Count As Integer
```

```
Private Sub cmdPick_Click()
Count = Count + 1
If (Count = 1) Then
Image1.Picture = LoadPicture("C:\vb\red.bmp")
ElseIf (Count = 2) Then
Image1.Picture = LoadPicture("C:\vb\green.bmp")
ElseIf (Count = 3) Then
Image1.Picture = LoadPicture("C:\vb\blue.bmp")
End If
If (Count = 3) Then
Count = 0
End If
End Sub
```

```
Private Sub cmdClear_Click()
Image1.Picture = LoadPicture("C:\vb\white.bmp")
Count = 0
End Sub
```

```
Private Sub cmdExit_Click()
End
End Sub
```

Code Listing 4.3 One button color selector

The variable called *Count* initializes with the value zero when the program first starts. It is immediately incremented each time the *Pick* button code runs. *If-Then* conditional statements are used where the values: 1 gives the color red, 2 is used for green, and 3 displays the color blue. Regular individual If-Then statements can be used, and you may wish to rewrite the code in that way, but it is a little bulkier. The counter variable is reinitialized to zero after the counter value of three, so that the program can go through the color sequence again from the beginning. The counter reset section of the code is shown as highlighted. We also highlighted the line that resets the counter in the clear subroutine, causing the color sequence to start at the beginning after the user clears the picture box.

Another method when a large number of conditional possibilities must be examined uses *Select Case* method, as shown in Code Listing 4.4. The only change from the previous code is in the *Pick* button section.

```
Dim Count As Integer
```

```
Private Sub cmdPick_Click()
Count = Count + 1
Select Case Count
Case 1: Image1.Picture = LoadPicture("C:\vb\red.bmp")
Case 2: Image1.Picture = LoadPicture("C:\vb\green.bmp")
Case 3: Image1.Picture = LoadPicture("C:\vb\blue.bmp")
End Select
If (Count = 3) Then
Count = 0
End If
End Sub
```

```
Private Sub cmdClear_Click()
Image1.Picture = LoadPicture("C:\vb\white.bmp")
Count = 0
End Sub
```

```
Private Sub cmdExit_Click()
End
End Sub
```

Code Listing 4.4 Select Case method of picking a color

The select case code is much more straight forward in instances when many possibilities must have responses. It would be even easier to see how cleaner this method would be if many more colors were to be displayed. We again have the sections highlighted where the counter is reset to start the color sequence at the beginning.

Section 4.4. Displaying Pictures with Option Buttons

A straightforward way to make a selection of a single image is to use the Option Button control. The check box control could also be used; however, check boxes allow for more than a singular choice. If we used check boxes in this program, we would have to limit the number of choices to only one in the code, whereas the option button is limited by default to only one choice. Sometimes option button controls are also referred to as radio buttons, and the form is displayed in Figure 4.4.

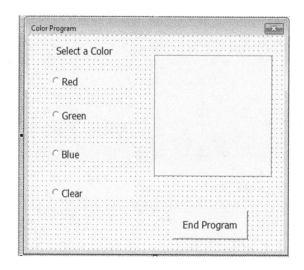

Figure 4.4 Option button color selection

When the user clicks an Option Button, the corresponding color is displayed. The standard naming convention uses the prefix, "opt", followed by a descriptive name for the control. We named them *optRed, optGreen, optBlue, and optClear* and changed their captions according to their colors in each control's properties box. In design mode, we double-clicked on each control on the form and coded the appropriate image to be loaded, as outlined in Code Listing 4.5.

```
Private Sub optRed_Click()
Image1.Picture = LoadPicture("C:\vb\red.bmp")
End Sub
```

```
Private Sub optGreen_Click()
Image1.Picture = LoadPicture("C:\vb\green.bmp")
End Sub
```

```
Private Sub optBlue_Click()
Image1.Picture = LoadPicture("C:\vb\blue.bmp")
End Sub
```

```
Private Sub optClear_Click()
Image1.Picture = LoadPicture("C:\vb\white.bmp")
End Sub
```

```
Private Sub cmdExit_Click()
End
End Sub
```

Code Listing 4.5 Option button color selection

Each option button directly loads a specific image when the user makes their selection. The *clear* button loads the white color, and the counter is no longer used, so the line resetting it to zero has been eliminated.

Section 4.5. Displaying Pictures with a List Box

List Boxes are helpful in instances where there are many options from which to choose. The clear button has been moved to now also become one of the selections in the list. The list box is populated at runtime, and Figure 4.5 shows the program form at design time.

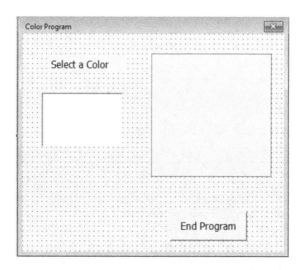

Figure 4.5 List box color selector

We use the Form Load event to populate the list. We are using Office 2016 version, and when double-clicking the blank form, it takes to the code for *UserForm_Click*, which must be manually changed to read *UserForm_Initialize*, as shown in the form code section of Code Listing 4.6. The selections that the user sees at runtime are then added to the code.

```
Private Sub UserForm_Initialize()
ListBox1.AddItem "Red"
ListBox1.AddItem "Green"
ListBox1.AddItem "Blue"
ListBox1.AddItem "Clear Screen"
End Sub
```

```
Private Sub ListBox1_Click()
Dim color As String
color = ListBox1.Text
Select Case color
Case "Red"
Image1.Picture = LoadPicture("C:\vb\red.bmp")
Case "Green"
Image1.Picture = LoadPicture("C:\vb\green.bmp")
Case "Blue"
Image1.Picture = LoadPicture("C:\vb\blue.bmp")
Case "Clear Screen"
Image1.Picture = LoadPicture("C:\vb\white.bmp")
End Select
End Sub
```

```
Private Sub cmdExit_Click()
End
End Sub
```

Code Listing 4.6 List Box color selector

We used the default name for the *List Box* and could have declared the variable *color* at the very top of the code in the general declarations section but decided to move it to the list box section for no specific reason. The variable can be used throughout the entire code as the type it is declared as in the general declaration section in the top section of the code. However, when listing a variable type in a private subroutine, the type that is specified only applies to that section of code. Also, when declaring a variable in a private subroutine, its value will not be retained outside of the subroutine. The advantage is not having to use functions to convert its type in other sections of code, if necessary. My personal preference is to declare all variables in the general section, but I wanted to point out the differences.

It is essential to observe capitalization in our code because the letter case must match precisely when comparing string data, as noted in the first project of the chapter. The *case select* condition displays a color in the image box when the user clicks the color name in the list box.

Section 4.6. Displaying Pictures with a Combo Box

The *combo box* is similar to the list box but requires less space on the form. A drop-down list of selections appears when the user clicks the drop-down arrow. The program form is shown in Figure 4.6.

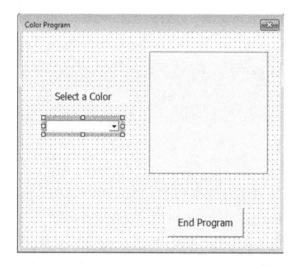

Figure 4.6 Combo box color selector

The items in the combo box are again populated during the Form_Initialize event. We used the default name for the combo box control. The code presented in Code Listing 4.7 is very similar to the code for the list box project but will provide a cleaner form at run-time.

```
Private Sub UserForm_Initialize()
ComboBox1.AddItem "Red"
ComboBox1.AddItem "Green"
```

```
ComboBox1.AddItem "Blue"
ComboBox1.AddItem "Clear Screen"
End Sub
```

```
Sub ComboBox1_Change()
Dim color As String
color = ComboBox1.Text
Select Case color
Case "Red"
Image1.Picture = LoadPicture("C:\vb\red.bmp")
Case "Green"
Image1.Picture = LoadPicture("C:\vb\green.bmp")
Case "Blue"
Image1.Picture = LoadPicture("C:\vb\blue.bmp")
Case "Clear Screen"
Image1.Picture = LoadPicture("C:\vb\white.bmp")
End Select
End Sub
```

```
Private Sub cmdExit_Click()
End
End Sub
```
Code Listing 4.7 Combo Box color selector

Section 4.7. Displaying Pictures with check boxes

Check boxes are not exclusive and allow for one or more possibilities. We cannot mix colors because the paths we take to display an image will only display one image at any given time. The form has now been altered to display three small image boxes. Although the color image is larger than the new boxes, a portion of the image will be displayed. The sizes were not matched in an effort to correspond with the other projects in the chapter. If you were displaying pictures rather than colors, the image box size and picture size would need to match. The new form appears in Figure 4.7.

47

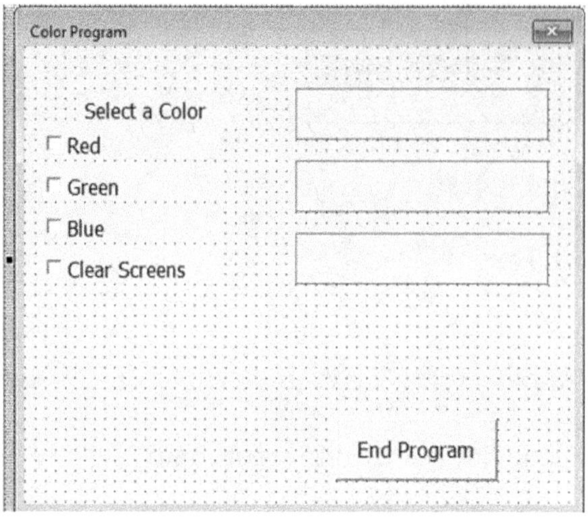

Figure 4.7 Check box color selector

The image boxes are named *imgRed, imgGreen, and imgBlue* from top-to-bottom. The check boxes are *chkRed, chkGreen, and chkBlue* with an additional check box to clear the colors named *chkClear*. Check boxes operate in a binary manner with a checked box equal to *True*, and no check in the box equal to *False*. When the form is cleared, the check boxes are unchecked by setting their value property to False as described in Code Listing 4.8.

```
Private Sub chkRed_Click()
imgRed.Picture = LoadPicture("C:\vb\red.bmp")
End Sub
```

```
Private Sub chkGreen_Click()
imgGreen.Picture = LoadPicture("C:\vb\green.bmp")
End Sub
```

```
Private Sub chkBlue_Click()
imgBlue.Picture = LoadPicture("C:\vb\blue.bmp")
End Sub
```

```
Private Sub chkClear_Click()
imgRed.Picture = LoadPicture("C:\vb\white.bmp")
imgGreen.Picture = LoadPicture("C:\vb\white.bmp")
imgBlue.Picture = LoadPicture("C:\vb\white.bmp")
chkRed.Value = False
chkGreen.Value = False
chkBlue.Value = False
Call Clear
End Sub
```
_____

```
Private Sub cmdExit_Click()
End
End Sub
```
_____

```
Public Sub Clear()                'added subroutine
If chkClear.Value = True Then
chkClear.Value = False
End If
End Sub
```
Code Listing 4.8 Check box color selector

An additional subroutine was added to reset the *clear colors* check box. Subroutines can be added to code by manually typing them and can be called from anywhere in the program by making them public, or just denoting them as *sub*. The end of the *clear colors* code calls the subroutine that we inserted to uncheck the clearing box, so the checkmark disappears.

Chapter Four Summary

Many of the controls in the toolbox were demonstrated and discussed. Using functions to convert text from a user to eliminate case mismatches were described. Some controls, such as the option button are exclusive, whereas check boxes can apply to more than one result. There are many functions built into the Visual Basic program, but we can add additional functionality by manually constructing public subroutines. This chapter's concentration was on images and pictures. Next, we will look into bringing multimedia files into our programs.

Chapter Five

Bringing Multimedia Files into a Program

Section 5.1. Producing Sounds with Option Buttons

This project's form is similar to Figure 4.4 in the last chapter, except now we added the Windows media player as displayed in Figure 5.1.

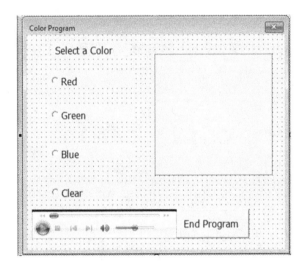

Figure 5.1. Option buttons with the Windows Media Player

If the media player is not found in the controls toolbox, right-click the toolbox or go to the tools menu and select it in the additional controls listing. You can then locate it anywhere on the form and set its visibility property to false so that it does not show on the form at run time. The code is a minor adaptation of the code Listing 4.5 of the last chapter. The additional lines of code to play the sounds are found in Code Listing 5.1.

```
Private Sub optRed_Click()
Image1.Picture = LoadPicture("C:\vb\red.bmp")
WindowsMediaPlayer1.URL = "C:\vb\chord.wav"
End Sub
```

```
Private Sub optGreen_Click()
Image1.Picture = LoadPicture("C:\vb\green.bmp")
WindowsMediaPlayer1.URL = "C:\vb\chord.wav"
End Sub


Private Sub optBlue_Click()
Image1.Picture = LoadPicture("C:\vb\blue.bmp")
WindowsMediaPlayer1.URL = "C:\vb\chord.wav"
End Sub


Private Sub optClear_Click()
Image1.Picture = LoadPicture("C:\vb\white.bmp")
WindowsMediaPlayer1.URL = "C:\vb\chord.wav"
End Sub


Private Sub cmdExit_Click()
End
End Sub
```

Code Listing 5.1. Option buttons for pictures and sound

In examining the additional code, we see that there are four instances where we call the Windows Media Player to open a .wav file at a URL. The location is on the local computer. The sound is found using the path C:\vb\chord.wav. It was copied there from its original Windows 10 location C:\windows\media\chord.wav. You can use the Windows direct path without using the VB folder, but it is convenient to have all the files for the programs in one location. Notice that the hierarchical separators use backslashes, unlike the forward-slashes used in Internet addresses. You may wish to add an additional sound to the exit button.

Section 5.2. Producing Sounds with Check Boxes

Chapter Four's last project is being modified to use a *Frame* as a container for the sound options available. The user can show or hide the sound controls to select sounds to accompany the color picture as it is displayed. We are leaving the default name for the frame but changing its caption to *Sounds*. Two option buttons are then added to the frame named *optChord* captioned as *Chord*, and *optChimes,* which has the caption *Chimes*. A control button is also added to the form called *cmdSounds* and captioned *Sound,* as shown in Figure 5.2.

Figure 5.2 Color and sound with check boxes

We are using the sound files that come with the Windows operating system. The show hidden files option must be enabled to see Windows files on the computer's C drive. We are copying two sound files to our VB folder containing our color pictures. The Windows 10 paths to the files are C:\windows\media\chord.wav, and C:\windows\media\chimes.wav. If you use other sounds or different paths, be sure to change the code accordingly. The Windows Media player was added to the form and made to fit in the frame. Its visible property is set to false, so the user does not see the player at run time. The modified code is similar to the last project in Chapter Four, with the changes shown as highlighted in Code Listing 5.2.

```
Dim chord As Boolean
```

```vb
Dim chimes As Boolean
Dim soundOn As Boolean

Private Sub chkRed_Click()
imgRed.Picture = LoadPicture("C:\vb\red.bmp")
If chord = True And soundOn = False Then
WindowsMediaPlayer1.URL = "C:\vb\chord.wav"
ElseIf chimes = True And soundOn = False Then
WindowsMediaPlayer1.URL = "C:\vb\chimes.wav"
End If
End Sub

Private Sub chkGreen_Click()
imgGreen.Picture = LoadPicture("C:\vb\green.bmp")
If chord = True And soundOn = False Then
WindowsMediaPlayer1.URL = "C:\vb\chord.wav"
ElseIf chimes = True And soundOn = False Then
WindowsMediaPlayer1.URL = "C:\vb\chimes.wav"
End If
End Sub

Private Sub chkBlue_Click()
imgBlue.Picture = LoadPicture("C:\vb\blue.bmp")
If chord = True And soundOn = False Then
WindowsMediaPlayer1.URL = "C:\vb\chord.wav"
ElseIf chimes = True And soundOn = False Then
WindowsMediaPlayer1.URL = "C:\vb\chimes.wav"
End If
End Sub

Private Sub chkClear_Click()
imgRed.Picture = LoadPicture("C:\vb\white.bmp")
imgGreen.Picture = LoadPicture("C:\vb\white.bmp")
imgBlue.Picture = LoadPicture("C:\vb\white.bmp")
chkRed.Value = False
chkGreen.Value = False
chkBlue.Value = False
```

```
Call Clear
End Sub
```

```
Private Sub cmdExit_Click()
End
End Sub
```

```
Public Sub Clear()
If chkClear.Value = True Then
chkClear.Value = False
End If
End Sub
```

```
Private Sub cmdSounds_Click() 'Sound button
Frame1.Visible = Not Frame1.Visible      'toggles on/off
soundOn = Not soundOn          'toggles variable
End Sub
```

```
Private Sub optChimes_Click()  'option button selector
chord = False
chimes = True
End Sub
```

```
Private Sub optchord_Click()     'option button selector
chord = True
chimes = False
End Sub
```

Code Listing 5.2 Color and sound with check boxes

As the sound button is clicked, both the frame visibility and the sound enabling variable *soundOn* are toggled. Identical *if/then else/If* compound conditional statements are used for each color check box where the AND logic ties both the *soundOn* enabling variable to the option button sound file selection. The variables are globally declared as Boolean, where they have two possibilities: *true* or *false*.

Section 5.3. Playing Songs

A variety of audio and video file types can be played by the Windows Media Player embedded in a VBA form. The project that we are working on now uses the player with its visible property set to *True*, allowing us to see the audio waves and use additional player controls, such as being able to adjust the volume. The form could also be streamlined to make the player not visible at run time, since the form can control the music selections. The list box will display songs available to be played, and the list can be updated and saved as pictured in Figure 5.3.

Figure 5.3 Music program

The list box is named *lstSongs* (Note: the first letter is a lower-case L, not a lower case I). The Text box is called *txtName*, and the buttons are *txtPlay, txtStop, txtAdd, txtDelete,* and *txtExit*. We use default names for the form, the labels, and the music player. The labels are captioned as shown. Label2 now showing stopped above the media player will display the song's path when playing. The code is given in Code Listing 5.3.

```
Private Sub cmdAdd_Click()
If Not txtName = "" Then
```

```
lstSongs.AddItem txtName.Text
Else
    MsgBox "Please Input Name"
    WindowsMediaPlayer1.URL = "C:\vb\chimes.wav"
End If
txtName = ""
End Sub
```

```
Private Sub cmdDelete_Click()
If lstSongs.ListIndex > -1 Then
    lstSongs.RemoveItem lstSongs.ListIndex
Else
    MsgBox "Please Highlight a Selection"
End If
End Sub
```

```
Private Sub cmdPlay_Click()
txtName.Text = lstSongs.Text
Dim X As String
Dim Y As String
X = txtName.Text 'song name
Y = "C:\vb\" & X 'path and song name
Label2 = Y & ".mp3" 'path, song name, and file extension
WindowsMediaPlayer1.URL = Y & ".mp3"
End Sub
```

```
Private Sub cmdStop_Click()
WindowsMediaPlayer1.URL = "C:\vb\chord.wav"
txtName.Text = ""
Label2 = "Stoped"
End Sub
```

```
Private Sub cmdExit_Click()
Dim NumSongs As Integer
Dim songs As String
Dim counter As Integer
Open "C:\vb\playlist.txt" For Output As #2
```

```
NumSongs = lstSongs.ListCount
For counter = 0 To NumSongs - 1
    songs = lstSongs.List(counter)
    Write #2, songs
Next
Close #2
End
End Sub
```

```
Public Sub UserForm_Initialize()
Dim Name As String
Open "C:\vb\playlist.txt" For Input As #1
Do Until EOF(1)
    Input #1, Name
    lstSongs.AddItem Name
Loop
Close #1
End Sub
```

Code Listing 5.3. Music player code

The add button uses the *addItem* method to add what the user types into the text box. If there is no text, a message box reminds the user to enter the name of a song to add. The delete button removes the list entry using the *removeItem* method and will display a message box asking the user to highlight the song that is to be deleted if one is not highlighted. Additional code could be added to also display an icon and the name of the program in the message box. The play button will start a song that is highlighted if it matches a song name located in the VB folder on the C drive. The user must save any .mp3 songs to be played in the folder, and then add them to the list in the program. The text must match exactly, although the upper or lower case does not matter. The text box displays the song that is playing, and the box will clear if the song is stopped.

The database consists of a text file which can be created using Notepad, found in the Windows Accessories programs of the *Start* menu. The text file must be named playlist.txt. The Notepad file will populate as song titles available are added to the playlist box at runtime, or can be added to the text file manually. Song titles are loaded in the list box from the Notepad file in the VB folder when the music program opens, and any changes are saved in the text file as the exit button is clicked. If the program is shut down without clicking the *Save and Exit* button, changes will not be saved.

My musical taste may not match yours, but I highly recommend the songs on my playlist. The program can be adapted to play recorded narrations, also .mp4 video files can be used with the Windows Media Player to display video presentations. Playing video files would require a path change in the play subroutine to specify .mp4 files. It would best have two play buttons, one for music like the one now, and add an additional button coded with the .mp4 extension for video files. You may need to change the Player to the default media player for your PC. You can do this by right-clicking on an .mp3 (or .mp4 file) and selecting the player with the *open with* command.

Chapter Five Summary

Sounds and video can be added to accompany user events by using the Windows Media Player. The player may need to be added from the selection of additional controls from the *tools* menu. The media player can be placed anywhere on the form, and the *visible* property set to *False* to make it invisible at run time, or it can be left with the default *True* property set so the user can see it. Just like loading picture files into an image box, the exact path must be used to locate the sound or video files. It is best to dedicate a file on the C drive to keep all multimedia files and program files in one location for convenience.

Chapter Six

Working with Numbers

Section 6.1. Adding Numbers

Up to this point, we have been using Word for all of the projects. We will now use Excel to add numbers on a VBA form. This book aims to have fun learning programming and not necessarily to use macros in Excel or other Office programs. We are only using Excel in this project to show that VBA works similarly in different Office programs. You can use Word and achieve the same results. The project form appears in Figure 6.1.

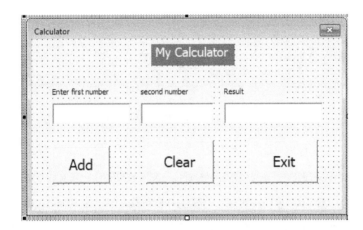

Figure 6.1 Calculator

A Background color is added to the label *My Calculator* in the properties window. You may also wish to add a foreground color to make the text stand out. Labels explain the purpose of the text boxes, and the default names are used since the labels do not have any code associated with them. The first text box is named *txtFirstNum*, the second is *txtSecondNum*, and the result text box is named *txtResult*. The code appears in Listing 6.1.

```
Dim firstNum As Double
Dim secondNum As Double
Dim result As Double


Private Sub cmdClear_Click()
txtFirstNum = ""
txtSecondNum = ""
txtResult = ""
End Sub


Private Sub cmdAdd_Click()
firstNum = CDbl(txtFirstNum.Text) 'converts to number
secondNum = CDbl(txtSecondNum.Text)
result = firstNum + secondNum
txtResult = CStr(result)    'converts back to text
End Sub


Private Sub cmdExit_Click()
End
End Sub
```

Code Listing 6.1 Addition calculator

The variables are declared as *double* precision since they can hold both whole and fractional amounts and have up to 15 significant digits. The work is all done when the user clicks the add button. The number entered into the first text box is converted from string data to a *double* by the CDbl() function built into the VB program. The same happens to the second text box. The two variables are then added and then converted back to the string data type, and then displayed in the result text box.

Some user issues can cause a bug. If a text box is left blank or a user inadvertently enters a character other than a number, the program will crash. The code next presented in Code Listing 6.2 addresses those issues with the new code highlighted.

```
Dim firstNum As Double
Dim secondNum As Double
Dim result As Double
```

```
Private Sub cmdClear_Click()
txtFirstNum = ""
txtSecondNum = ""
txtResult = ""
End Sub
```

```
Private Sub cmdAdd_Click()
If IsNumeric(txtFirstNum.Text) Then
firstNum = CDbl(txtFirstNum.Text)
   Else
   MsgBox ("Please check first number")
   End If
If IsNumeric(txtSecondNum.Text) Then
secondNum = CDbl(txtSecondNum.Text)
   Else
   MsgBox ("Please check second number")
   End If
result = firstNum + secondNum
txtResult = CStr(result)
End Sub
```

```
Private Sub cmdExit_Click()
End
End Sub
```

Code Listing 6.2 Addition calculator bug fix

The user input is tested to make sure it is numeric by the built-in function *IsNumeric* (). If the user inputs are proper, then the text box inputs are converted to the double data type, and the result of the addition is converted back and displayed as string data. Troubleshooting to find bugs and developing fixes is a challenging but essential part of programming. Ease of use is also an important part of creating a program. We should have the first text box *tab* property set to zero, the second set to one, and the *Add* button tab should be 2. (The tabs are set in the properties window and start at zero.) The setting will allow the user to immediately type a number in the first box and use the keyboard enter or tab button to get to the second text box. They then can enter the second number and get the result by pressing enter. One of the great advantages of Visual Basic is that many attributes and program flow can be set in the properties box without the need for coding the actions.

Section 6.2. Adding, Subtracting, Multiplying, and Dividing

We will expand the functionality of the calculator program to perform the four basic arithmetic operations. The button to sum the first and second number is named *cmdSum*, subtract is *cmdSubtract*, multiply is *cmdMultiply*, and divide is called *cmdDivide*. The text boxes are *txtFirstNumber*, *txtSecondNumber*, and *txtAnswer*. The other buttons are *cmdClear* and *cmdExit,* as shown in the form in Figure 6.2. It is good practice to start the name with the three-letter abbreviation of the control, followed by a descriptive name.

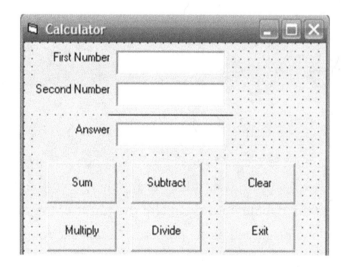

Figure 6.2 Basic calculator

```vbnet
Dim First As Double
Dim Second As Double
Dim Sum As Double
```

```vbnet
Private Sub cmdClear_Click()
txtFirstNumber = " "
txtSecondNumber = " "
txtAnswer = " "
End Sub
```

```vbnet
Private Sub cmdExit_Click()
End
End Sub
```

```vbnet
'The code to sum
Private Sub cmdSum_Click()
If Not IsNumeric(txtFirstNumber.Text) Then
    MsgBox ("Enter First Number")
    txtAnswer.Text = ""
    txtFirstNumber.Text = ""
    txtFirstNumber.SetFocus        'puts cursor in the first text box

ElseIf Not IsNumeric(txtSecondNumber.Text) Then
    MsgBox ("Enter Second Number")
    txtAnswer.Text = ""
    txtSecondNumber.Text = ""
    txtSecondNumber.SetFocus     'puts cursor in the second text box

Else
    First = CDbl(txtFirstNumber.Text)
    Second = CDbl(txtSecondNumber.Text)
    Sum = First + Second
    txtAnswer.Text = CStr(Sum)
'I call the answer variable sum
End If
End Sub
```

```
'Code to subtract
Private Sub cmdSubtract_Click()
If Not IsNumeric(txtFirstNumber.Text) Then
    MsgBox ("Enter First Number")
    txtAnswer.Text = ""
    txtFirstNumber.Text = ""
    txtFirstNumber.SetFocus

ElseIf Not IsNumeric(txtSecondNumber.Text) Then
    MsgBox ("Enter Second Number")
    txtAnswer.Text = ""
    txtSecondNumber.Text = ""
    txtSecondNumber.SetFocus

Else
    First = CDbl(txtFirstNumber.Text)
    Second = CDbl(txtSecondNumber.Text)
    Sum = First - Second
    txtAnswer.Text = CStr(Sum)

End If
End Sub
```

```
'The code to divide
Private Sub cmdDivide_Click()
If Not IsNumeric(txtFirstNumber.Text) Then
    MsgBox ("Enter First Number")
    txtAnswer.Text = ""
    txtFirstNumber.Text = ""
    txtFirstNumber.SetFocus

ElseIf Not IsNumeric(txtSecondNumber.Text) Then
    MsgBox ("Enter Second Number")
    txtAnswer.Text = ""
    txtSecondNumber.Text = ""
    txtSecondNumber.SetFocus
ElseIf txtSecondNumber.Text = 0 Then
```

```
        MsgBox ("Division by zero is not nice")
        txtAnswer.Text = ""
        txtSecondNumber.Text = ""
        txtSecondNumber.SetFocus

Else
First = CDbl(txtFirstNumber.Text)
        Second = CDbl(txtSecondNumber.Text)
        Sum = First / Second
        txtAnswer.Text = CStr(Sum)

End If
End Sub
```

```
'Code to multiply
Private Sub cmdMultiply_Click()
If Not IsNumeric(txtFirstNumber.Text) Then
        MsgBox ("Enter First Number")
        txtAnswer.Text = ""
        txtFirstNumber.Text = ""
        txtFirstNumber.SetFocus

ElseIf Not IsNumeric(txtSecondNumber.Text) Then
        MsgBox ("Enter Second Number")
        txtAnswer.Text = ""
        txtSecondNumber.Text = ""
        txtSecondNumber.SetFocus

Else
        First = CDbl(txtFirstNumber.Text)
        Second = CDbl(txtSecondNumber.Text)
        Sum = First * Second
        txtAnswer.Text = CStr(Sum)

End If
End Sub
```

Code Listing 6.3. Four function calculator

The coding for each arithmetic operation is a similar process of first checking to make sure the user has entered numbers correctly before converting the text box inputs into the *double* number type and storing them in the variables named *first* and *second*. The second text box number is also checked during the division process so that it is not zero or a message box pops up. The answer is converted back to a string and written in the text box after the calculation. *Set focus* directs the cursor to a convenient location after an operation to make the program run smoothly for the user.

Section 6.3. Basic calculator with buttons.

Most calculators use keys to input numbers, which are then displayed on a screen. The math operation is keyed in, and then the second number is input. Pressing the equal key will perform the operation and display the result. The form that we built for this project is shown in Figure 6.3.

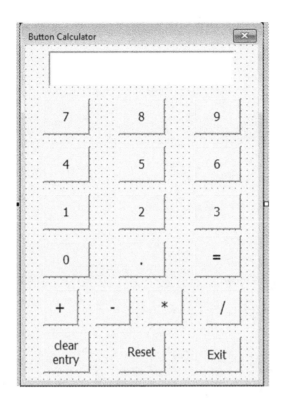

Figure 6.3

This program provides the four basic arithmetic operations using the button names *cmdAdd*, *cmdSubtract, cmdMultiply, and cmdDivide*. The number buttons are named using the cmd prefix followed by each spelled-out number, such as *cmdZero*. The other buttons are named *cmdClear, cmdReset, and cmdExit*. The default names are used for both the text box and form. Code Listing 6.3 shows the basic calculator program for this project.

```
Dim leftSide As String
Dim subTotal As Double
Dim operation As String
Dim answerValue As Double
```

```vb
Private Sub cmdPoint_Click()
leftSide = TextBox1.Text
TextBox1.Text = leftSide & "."
End Sub


Private Sub cmdNine_Click()
leftSide = TextBox1.Text
TextBox1.Text = leftSide & "9"
End Sub


Private Sub cmdEight_Click()
leftSide = TextBox1.Text
TextBox1.Text = leftSide & "8"
End Sub


Private Sub cmdSeven_Click()
leftSide = TextBox1.Text
TextBox1.Text = leftSide & "7"
End Sub


Private Sub cmdSix_Click()
leftSide = TextBox1.Text
TextBox1.Text = leftSide & "6"
End Sub


Private Sub cmdFive_Click()
leftSide = TextBox1.Text
TextBox1.Text = leftSide & "5"
End Sub


Private Sub cmdFour_Click()
leftSide = TextBox1.Text
TextBox1.Text = leftSide & "4"
End Sub


Private Sub cmdThree_Click()
leftSide = TextBox1.Text
```

```vb
TextBox1.Text = leftSide & "3"
End Sub


Private Sub cmdTwo_Click()
leftSide = TextBox1.Text
TextBox1.Text = leftSide & "2"
End Sub


Private Sub cmdOne_Click()
leftSide = TextBox1.Text
TextBox1.Text = leftSide & "1"
End Sub


Private Sub cmdZero_Click()
If operation = "Divide" Then
MsgBox ("Can't Divide by zero")
TextBox1 = ""
leftSide = 0
operation = ""
answerValue = 0
subTotal = 0
Else
leftSide = TextBox1.Text
TextBox1.Text = leftSide & "0"
End If
End Sub


Private Sub cmdAdd_Click()
If Not TextBox1.Text = "" Then
subTotal = CDbl(TextBox1.Text) + subTotal
operation = "Add"
TextBox1 = ""
End If
End Sub


Private Sub cmdSubtract_Click()
If Not TextBox1.Text = "" Then
```

```vb
subTotal = CDbl(TextBox1.Text) + subTotal
operation = "Subtract"
TextBox1 = ""
End If
End Sub
```

```vb
Private Sub cmdMultiply_Click()
If Not TextBox1.Text = "" Then
subTotal = CDbl(TextBox1.Text) + subTotal
operation = "Multiply"
TextBox1 = ""
End If
End Sub
```

```vb
Private Sub cmdDivide_Click()
If Not TextBox1.Text = "" Then
subTotal = CDbl(TextBox1.Text) + subTotal
operation = "Divide"
TextBox1 = ""
End If
End Sub
```

```vb
Private Sub cmdAnswer_Click()
If Not TextBox1.Text = "" Then 'nested if checks for 2nd num input
If operation = "Add" Then
answerValue = subTotal + CDbl(TextBox1.Text)
TextBox1.Text = CStr(answerValue)
ElseIf operation = "Subtract" Then
answerValue = subTotal - CDbl(TextBox1.Text)
TextBox1.Text = CStr(answerValue)
ElseIf operation = "Multiply" Then
answerValue = subTotal * CDbl(TextBox1.Text)
TextBox1.Text = CStr(answerValue)

ElseIf operation = "Divide" Then
answerValue = subTotal / CDbl(TextBox1.Text)
TextBox1.Text = CStr(answerValue)
```

```
End If 'inner nest end
subTotal = 0
End If 'outer nest end
End Sub
```

```
Private Sub cmdClear_Click()
TextBox1 = ""
End Sub
```

```
Private Sub cmdReset_Click()
TextBox1 = ""
leftSide = 0
operation = ""
answerValue = 0
subTotal = 0
End Sub
```

```
Private Sub cmdExit_Click()
End
End Sub
```

Code Listing 6.3. Button calculator

The coding for numbers one through nine and the decimal point is repetitious can be copied and pasted with the specific digit's updated information. All variable types in the program are strings and doubles. The variable *leftSide* is a string type variable that can be concatenated, as multiple digit numbers are input. An *if/then* check is made in the zero section so that division by zero will not be allowed. Each section of the arithmetic operators check that the user has input the second number before converting the text box input to a *double* type, and saving the *string* type name of the operation to the string variable named *operation*. The *equals* sign uses nested *if/then* conditional statements to make sure the user entered a second number. Then the inside section matches the string name using *if/then else/if* conditional matches to perform the mathematical operation. The result is then converted back to the *string* data type and displayed in the text box. The clear button can clear the text box if the user entered an incorrect number. The reset button clears the text box and all variables so the user can run a new computation from the beginning.

Chapter Six Summary

We saw how to add numbers in the first project and then went on to produce a four-function arithmetic calculator program. Built-in VB functions were used to convert between data types so that numbers could be input and output from text boxes. The *double* data type was used for calculations since it can hold very large numbers and works with fractional values involving the decimal point. We produced a well-functioning button type calculator program similar to the calculator accessory app included with many computer operating systems. Next, we will have fun with numbers and learn to generate random values.

Chapter Seven

Random Numbers

Section 7.1. The Random Number Generator

A realistic random number is challenging to generate. One of the simplest ways to create a pseudo-random number, using digital electronics hardware, is to stop a fast running number counter at a random time. This method is used in many low-cost games, but the timing can become somewhat predictable if the game is played for long periods. With software, a pseudo-random number can be formed with an arithmetic process using division and examining remainders. In areas of science and mathematics, there are complex mathematical algorithms that can be employed when a very random number is needed. Visual Basic has a pseudo-random number generator using a software timer as a seed and code to limit the band of numbers to be chosen. A basic random number generator form appears in Figure 7.1.

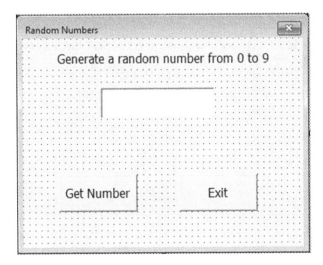

Figure 7.1. Random number generator

The code for generating and displaying a random number is contained in the subroutine for the *Get Number* button named *cmdGetNumber*. The text box is named *txtOutput*. In Code Listing 7.1, we pick and display a random number from zero through nine; the number generation code is highlighted. (Note: the character between *Rnd* and 10 is an asterisk.)

```
Private Sub cmdGetNumber_Click()
Dim x As Integer
Randomize Timer
x = Int(Rnd * 10)          '0 through 9 is 10 possibilities
txtOutput.Text = CStr(x)
End Sub
```

```
Private Sub cmdExit_Click()
End
End Sub
```

Code Listing 7.1

Computers start counting at zero. They include the zero value, whereas humans start counting at one. After we declare the variable x as an integer, we randomize the number between zero and 9 (10 possibilities). The variable is converted from an integer to the string data type, which is to be displayed in the output text box. We may want to start our program number range at one. The highlighted section can be modified, as shown in Code Listing 7.2.

```
Randomize Timer
x = Int(Rnd * 9) + 1
```

Code Listing 7.2

By adding one to the variable x, we eliminate the chance of the number being zero, and we change the total number of possibilities.

Section 7.2. Non-duplicate Random Numbers

In testing the program in the last section, we find that the randomness doesn't seem to be very good because the range of numbers is small, and some of the numbers tend to repeat. We can make an adjustment in the code to not allow for too much repetition. The revised code appears in Listing 7.2.

```
Dim x As Integer
Dim lastNumber As Integer


Private Sub cmdGetNumber_Click()
Repeat:            'repeat section start
Randomize Timer
x = Int(Rnd * 10) + 1
If x = lastNumber Then
GoTo Repeat     'if a dupe, repeats the section
End If
lastNumber = x
txtOutput.Text = CStr(x)
End Sub


Private Sub cmdExit_Click()
End
End Sub
```
Code Listing 7.3 Non-duplicate numbers

If the random number happens to be a repeat, the code uses a bit of an unorthodox method of jumping backward using the *GoTo* command to the *label* called *Repeat*. The variables are now moved to the public general declaration section, so their values are retained between clicks. The variable *lastNumber* must have its value from the end of the subroutine maintained, so the next time through it can be evaluated to ensure it does not match the new *x* variable's value. This method is one way to stop any repeating of the random numbers and seems to help produce a better selection. A more robust process could examine more than just the last number in the sequence. Our next iteration will look at eliminating duplication at a greater distance.

We are still using the original form of Figure 7.1, but now we are using a little more complex algorithm to cut back on number duplication. The code from Listing 7.3 is now being modified to use a loop for replacing recently derived numbers, and the code appears in Listing 7.4.

```
Dim x As Integer
Dim timesThrough As Integer
Dim counter As Integer
Dim number(5) As Integer
```

```
Private Sub cmdGetNumber_Click()
Repeat: 'repeat section start
Randomize Timer
x = Int(Rnd * 10) + 1
For counter = 0 To 4 Step 1     'loop for dupes
If x = number(counter) Then
GoTo Repeat 'if a dupe, repeats the section
End If
Next counter     'loops up from here 5X
number(timesThrough) = x
txtOutput.Text = CStr(x)
timesThrough = timesThrough + 1
If timesThrough > 4 Then
timesThrough = 0
End If
End Sub
```

```
Private Sub cmdExit_Click()
End
End Sub
```

Code Listing 7.4 Spacing repeating numbers

The general declaration section for the new variable we are now using called *number* is for an array. Arrays use the same variable to hold many different values and are organized by a subscript number following the variable. We are declaring 5 as the subscript, which gives a maximum number of elements in the array of 5, with subscripts 0 through 4. This process will allow us to separate numbers to not repeat more than once in every 5 picks. This number has been arbitrarily chosen for our current project. Just as in the code of listing 7.3, we will use a *goto* command to rerun the random number generator when a number match exists. However, we are now looking as far back as five numbers. This process is using a *for/next* loop. The first line in the loop, *For counter = 0 To 4*, initializes the variable called *counter* at zero, and the next part of the line of code, *Step 1* will increment the count each time it goes through the loop. The bottom of the loop is the line of code that says *Next counter*. This process ensures that if the current number generated matches any of the last five digits, it is regenerated and stored as the next number in the random sequence. *For/next* counters are used mainly when a specific number of iterations must be performed. Other loop methods use *do while* and *until* determiners to spin through the loop until a condition is met.

The five times for *next loop* check eliminates nearby repeating numbers and makes the process seem more random. It is also possible to increase the range of numbers to pick from to help eliminate duplication. It may be interesting to modify this project to generate random numbers with a larger range of perhaps between one and one hundred.

Chapter Seven Summary

Generating a pseudo-random number requires a seed, and the range of numbers must be specified. In Visual Basic, the code *Randomize Timer* seeds the process, and the code *Rnd* and the maximum number are separated with an asterisk. We used the code Int(Rnd * 9) + 1 to create a random integer of one to nine. A *For/next* loop was used to eliminate duplication of the numbers. Many other methods can be used for creating loops, *For/next* are useful when a preset number around the loop is known. Other loop methods include *While* and *Do* loops. The old and slightly more cumbersome method of *goto* a *label* will be utilized in the next chapter as we use random numbers in games.

Chapter Eight

Games with Random Numbers

Section 8.1. Higher or Lower Game

This game uses two buttons to get randomly generated numbers between 0 and 100. The user clicks a button for the first number of the game to appear, and then uses option buttons to select their guess as to if the second randomly generated number will be higher or lower than the first. The form is in figure 8.1.

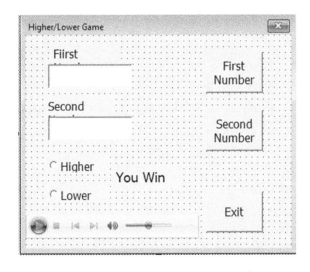

Figure 8.1 Higher/Lower game

The Windows Media Player is on the form with its property set to *not visible,* and the chime sound plays when the user wins, the chord plays on a loss. The label's name for the text boxes use the default names but are captioned in the properties window as *First* and *Second*. The command buttons are named *cmdFirst*, *cmdSecond*, and *cmdExit*. The option buttons are named *optHigher* and *optLower* and captioned accordingly. The third label is named *lblWinner,* and its caption is changed during the running of the game to display winning and losing messages. The code appears in Code Listing 8.1.

```
Dim counter As Integer
Dim firstNumber As Integer
Dim secondNumber As Integer
Dim higher As Boolean
Dim lower As Boolean
```

```
Private Sub cmdFirst_Click()
If counter = 0 Then
Randomize Timer
firstNumber = Int(Rnd * 101)
txtFirstNumber.Text = Str(firstNumber)
txtSecondNumber.Text = ""
Else
MsgBox "Please pick a second number"
End If
counter = 1
End Sub
```

```
Private Sub cmdSecond_Click()
If counter = 1 Then
Randomize Timer
secondNumber = (Rnd * 101)
txtSecondNumber.Text = Str(secondNumber)
Else
MsgBox "Please pick a first number"
End If
If (higher = True) And (secondNumber > firstNumber) Then
lblWinner.Caption = "You Win !!!"
WindowsMediaPlayer1.URL = "C:\vb\chimes.wav"
ElseIf (higher = True) And (firstNumber > secondNumber) Then
lblWinner.Caption = "You Lose"
WindowsMediaPlayer1.URL = "C:\vb\chord.wav"
ElseIf (lower = True) And (secondNumber > firstNumber) Then
```

```
lblWinner.Caption = "You Lose"
WindowsMediaPlayer1.URL = "C:\vb\chord.wav"
ElseIf (lower = True) And (firstNumber > secondNumber) Then
lblWinner.Caption = "You Win !!!"
WindowsMediaPlayer1.URL = "C:\vb\chimes.wav"
End If
counter = 0
higher = False
lower = False
optHigher = 0
optLower = 0
End Sub
```

```
Private Sub optHigher_Click()
If counter = 0 Then        'haven't picked first number
MsgBox ("Please pick first number")
optHigher = 0              'clears option button
Else
higher = 1
lower = 0
End If
End Sub
```

```
Private Sub optLower_Click()
If counter = 0 Then       'haven't picked first number
MsgBox ("Please pick first number")
optLower = 0     'clears option button
Else
higher = 0
lower = 1
End If
End Sub
```

```
Private Sub cmdExit_Click()
End
End Sub
```

Code Listing 8.1 Higher/Lower game

Clicking the start button begins the game, and the first number is displayed. If the user clicks the second button first, a message box tells them to click the first button. The variable called *counter* is used to keep track of the order of button clicks. *Counter* becomes 1 after the first random number is displayed in the first text box. We could have given it the Boolean data type in the general declarations section since it only has two possibilities. The option buttons are set at Boolean types since they are true or false, depending on the user's choice after the first number appears. The majority of the heavy lifting is done in the second number code. If the button sequence using the counter variable is correct, the variables *firstNumber* and *secondNumber* are tested using *if/then else/if* conditions, and the option button selection, to determine a win or loss with the message appearing on the label, also the appropriate .wav file sound is made. Notice that since we have expanded the range of numbers in this game, now the code from the last chapter to eliminate duplicate random numbers is no longer needed. You may wish to add it, however, to make the feel of randomization even better.

There is some error checking built into the code in this project. A counter is used so that the player cannot choose a higher/lower option before the first number is picked, and as we mentioned earlier, they can't pick the second number before picking the first. We must always be aware that a user can bug-up a program, and we write safeguards into the code. Throughout other coding examples, we may not do this since the main objective is how to code, but if you are writing a program for the general public, you should keep safeguards in mind.

Section 8.2. One-button Higher/lower Game with Score

This section demonstrates some slightly different coding procedures and expands on the game in Section 8.1 to include scorekeeping and interactive messages. The failsafe code for user misuse is neglected for brevity. With more interactivity in this version, the user experience is more natural. We have included message box popups that may not be necessary and may be removed. The user form now only uses one button, as shown in Figure 8.2.

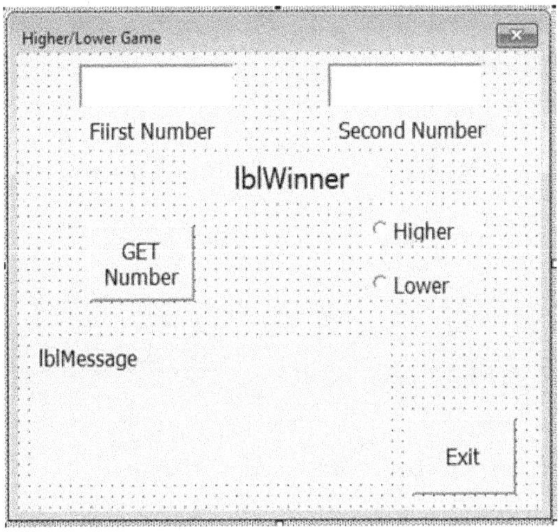

Figure 8.2 One button higher/lower game

The option button properties of *optHigher* and *optLower* are set to *not visible* at run time. They are made visible at the appropriate time with coding. Many other objects remain named the same as in the last project, such as *txtFirstNumber, txtSecondNumber, and lblWinner*. A new label named *lblMessage* has been added to display the score. The single button is named *cmdGetNumber,* and the code for the two buttons of the last project have been combined and modified as outlined in Code Listing 8.2.

```
Dim counter As Integer
Dim firstNumber As Integer
Dim secondNumber As Integer
Dim higher As Integer
Dim lower As Integer
Dim score As Integer
Dim total As Integer
Dim win As Integer
```

```
Private Sub cmdGetNumber_Click()
```

```
If counter = 0 Then
lblWinner = "Game in Play"
optHigher.Visible = True
optLower.Visible = True
Randomize
firstNumber = Int((99 * Rnd) + 1)
txtFirstNumber.Text = Str(firstNumber)
txtSecondNumber = ""
Randomize
secondNumber = Int((99 * Rnd) + 1)
counter = 1
End If

If counter = 1 Then
If (higher = 1) And (secondNumber > firstNumber) Then
win = 1
lblWinner.Caption = "You Win !!!"
txtSecondNumber.Text = Str(secondNumber)
score = 1
total = total + score
lblMessage = "Your Score is " + Str(total) & ("  Play again?")
counter = 0
lower = 0
higher = 0
optHigher.Value = 0
optLower.Value = 0
optHigher.Visible = False
optLower.Visible = False

ElseIf (higher = 1) And (firstNumber > secondNumber) Then
win = 0
lblWinner = "You lose"
txtSecondNumber.Text = Str(secondNumber)
score = -1
total = total + score
lblMessage = "Your Score is " + Str(total) & ("  Play again?")
counter = 0
```

```
lower = 0
higher = 0
optHigher.Value = 0
optLower.Value = 0
optHigher.Visible = False
optLower.Visible = False

ElseIf (lower = 1) And (firstNumber > secondNumber) Then
win = 1
lblWinner = "You Win"
txtSecondNumber.Text = Str(secondNumber)
score = 1
total = total + score
lblMessage = "Your Score is " + Str(total) & ("  Play again?")
counter = 0
lower = 0
higher = 0
optHigher.Value = 0
optLower.Value = 0
optHigher.Visible = False
optLower.Visible = False

ElseIf (lower = 1) And (secondNumber > firstNumber) Then
win = 0
lblWinner = "You Lose"
txtSecondNumber.Text = Str(secondNumber)
score = -1
total = total + score
lblMessage = "Your Score is " + Str(total) & ("  Play again?")
counter = 0
lower = 0
higher = 0
optHigher.Value = 0
optLower.Value = 0
optHigher.Visible = False
optLower.Visible = False
```

```
ElseIf (firstNumber = secondNumber) Then
win = 0
lblWinner = "A Draw"
txtSecondNumber.Text = Str(secondNumber)
score = 0
total = total + score
lblMessage = "Your Score is " + Str(total) & ("  Play again?")
counter = 0
lower = 0
higher = 0
optHigher.Value = 0
optLower.Value = 0
optHigher.Visible = False
optLower.Visible = False
End If
End If
If (total = -3) And (win = 0) Then
MsgBox "you're not very lucky", vbCritical, "Loser"
win = 1
ElseIf (total = -5) And (win = 0) Then
MsgBox "Give it up", vbCritical, "Loser"
win = 1
End If
End Sub
```

```
Private Sub optHigher_Click()
If counter = 1 Then
higher = 1
lower = 0
End If
End Sub
```

```
Private Sub optLower_Click()
If counter = 1 Then
higher = 0
lower = 1
End If
```

```
End Sub
```

```
Private Sub cmdExit_Click()
End
End Sub
```

Code Listing 8.2 One button higher/lower game

Both random numbers are generated when the player starts the round by clicking the button. The first number is displayed, and the second text box is cleared from any previous play. The play counter is set to one which sets both option buttons visible property to *true*. With the play counter set to one, the next button click will display the second number and uses AND logic in the conditional *if/then else/if* statements to determine a win or loss. The score is a positive one for a correct guess, and a negative one if incorrect. The score of the round is added to the total score. *lblWinner* displays a win or a loss, and the score information is displayed on the label *lblLabel*. After a loss with a total score of minus three, a nasty message box pops up. This reoccurs at a total score of minus five. The message boxes are a bit annoying, and you may wish to delete that section of code.

Section 8.3. One-button Game with Odds

It's not a good idea to trust computer games, always to be fair. Sometimes the programmer of a game could add some nefarious code that generates a skewed result. Using the same project in the last section of the chapter, we are adjusting the first part in the *cmdGetNumber* area and rewriting the two possible winning sections, as highlighted in Code Listing 8.3.

```
Private Sub cmdGetNumber_Click()
If counter = 0 Then
lblWinner = "Game in Play"
optHigher.Visible = True
```

```
optLower.Visible = True
Randomize
firstNumber = Int((99 * Rnd) + 1)
txtFirstNumber.Text = Str(firstNumber)
txtSecondNumber = ""
cheat:      'if win, restarts here
Randomize
secondNumber = Int((99 * Rnd) + 1)
counter = 1
…


If counter = 1 Then
If (higher = 1) And (secondNumber > firstNumber) Then
GoTo cheat
…


ElseIf (lower = 1) And (firstNumber > secondNumber) Then
GoTo cheat
```

Code Listing 8.3 Cheat code

The *goto* looping back to the random second number generation section anytime the player should have won the game ensures that they will never win. At best, the player may achieve a tie with no score. We can make the cheating less obvious while still tilting the odds in favor of the game with the modification of the original code in the last section with areas modified now as highlighted and presented in Code Listing 8.4.

```
 Dim counter As Integer
Dim firstNumber As Integer
Dim secondNumber As Integer
Dim higher As Integer
Dim lower As Integer
Dim score As Integer
Dim total As Integer
Dim win As Integer
Dim cheatcounter As Integer
```

```
Private Sub cmdGetNumber_Click()
If counter = 0 Then
lblWinner = "Game in Play"
optHigher.Visible = True
optLower.Visible = True
Randomize
firstNumber = Int((99 * Rnd) + 1)
txtFirstNumber.Text = Str(firstNumber)
txtSecondNumber = ""
Cheat:
cheatcounter = cheatcounter + 1   'starts at one
If cheatcounter > 10 Then   'resets on 11
cheatcounter = 1            'has values resets
End If
Randomize
secondNumber = Int((99 * Rnd) + 1)
counter = 1
...

If counter = 1 Then
If (higher = 1) And (secondNumber > firstNumber) Then
If cheatcounter < 4 Then '3 cheat loops (30 percent)
GoTo Cheat
End If
...

ElseIf (lower = 1) And (firstNumber > secondNumber) Then
If cheatcounter < 4 Then '3 cheat loops (30 percent)
GoTo Cheat
End If
```

Code Listing 8.4 Tipping the odds

The code will still allow the player to win, especially when the first number is near the extreme ends of the range. This can be compensated by adding extra code so that more cheat loops occur if the first number is toward the edges of the number range. The code in Listing 8.4 is mild in that the cheat loop is only three times out of a count of ten. This type of odds setting seems reasonable to the player, and they may not realize the game has odds against them. Our next project lets the player set the difficulty level.

Section 8.4. One-button Higher/lower Game with Levels

A combo box is added to the user form to allow a selection of the level of difficulty. We are making the code more concise by picking a random number in the first section, and a second random number with the cheat code are both together in the second section. The form is similar to the one-button design appearing in Figure 8.2. However, a combo box has been added, named *cboLevel*. All other names from before are being reused. The modified form appears in Figure 8.3.

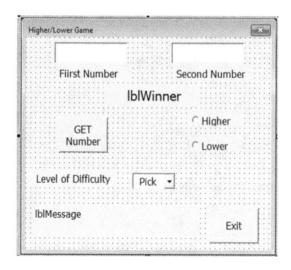

Figure 8.3 Higher/Lower game with levels of difficulty

The *caption* property of the combo box is *Pick*, and it appears at start-up, but when a user clicks the combo box dropdown arrow, the choices of *Easy, Medium, and Hard* show in the box. They are loaded at run time in the UserForm_Initialize() Public Subroutine. This is a similar method to how we populated the DJ playlist in Section 5.3. However, since this project's choices are static and will not change, we use the *addItem* method to load them directly from the code at runtime. The entire code is in Listing 8.5.

```
Dim counter As Integer
Dim firstNumber As Integer
Dim secondNumber As Integer
Dim higher As Integer
Dim lower As Integer
Dim score As Integer
Dim total As Integer
Dim win As Integer
Dim cheatcounter As Integer
Dim level As String
Dim difficulty As Integer
```

```
Private Sub cboLevel_Change()
level = cboLevel.Text   'loads the level variable from combo box
End Sub
```

```
Private Sub cmdGetNumber_Click()
If counter = 0 Then
counter = 1
lblWinner = "Game in Play"
optHigher.Visible = True
optLower.Visible = True
Randomize
firstNumber = Int((99 * Rnd) + 1)
txtFirstNumber.Text = Str(firstNumber)
txtSecondNumber = ""
End If  'End of first number

If counter = 1 Then     'Start second section

If level = "Easy" Then  'This comes from combo box
```

```
difficulty = 1
ElseIf level = "Medium" Then
difficulty = 3
ElseIf level = "Hard" Then
difficulty = 6
Else
difficulty = 9
End If

Cheat:
cheatcounter = cheatcounter + 1 'starts at one
If cheatcounter > 10 Then   'resets on 11
cheatcounter = 1
End If

Randomize
secondNumber = Int((99 * Rnd) + 1)
If (higher = 1) And (secondNumber > firstNumber) Then

If cheatcounter < difficulty Then   'cbo level
GoTo Cheat
End If

win = 1
lblWinner.Caption = "You Win !!!"
txtSecondNumber.Text = Str(secondNumber)
score = 1
total = total + score
lblMessage = "Your Score is " + Str(total) & ("  Play again?")
counter = 0
lower = 0
higher = 0
optHigher.Value = 0
optLower.Value = 0
optHigher.Visible = False
optLower.Visible = False
cheatcounter = 0
```

```
ElseIf (higher = 1) And (firstNumber > secondNumber) Then
win = 0
lblWinner = "You lose"
txtSecondNumber.Text = Str(secondNumber)
score = -1
total = total + score
lblMessage = "Your Score is " + Str(total) & ("  Play again?")
counter = 0
lower = 0
higher = 0
optHigher.Value = 0
optLower.Value = 0
optHigher.Visible = False
optLower.Visible = False
cheatcounter = 0


ElseIf (lower = 1) And (firstNumber > secondNumber) Then


If cheatcounter < difficulty Then   'cbo level
GoTo Cheat
End If


win = 1
lblWinner = "You Win"
txtSecondNumber.Text = Str(secondNumber)
score = 1
total = total + score
lblMessage = "Your Score is " + Str(total) & ("  Play again?")
counter = 0
lower = 0
higher = 0
optHigher.Value = 0
optLower.Value = 0
optHigher.Visible = False
optLower.Visible = False
cheatcounter = 0
ElseIf (lower = 1) And (secondNumber > firstNumber) Then
```

```
win = 0
lblWinner = "You Lose"
txtSecondNumber.Text = Str(secondNumber)
score = -1
total = total + score
lblMessage = "Your Score is " + Str(total) & ("  Play again?")
counter = 0
lower = 0
higher = 0
optHigher.Value = 0
optLower.Value = 0
optHigher.Visible = False
optLower.Visible = False
cheatcounter = 0

ElseIf (firstNumber = secondNumber) Then
win = 0
lblWinner = "A Draw"
txtSecondNumber.Text = Str(secondNumber)
score = 0
total = total + score
lblMessage = "Your Score is " + Str(total) & ("  Play again?")
counter = 0
lower = 0
higher = 0
optHigher.Value = 0
optLower.Value = 0
optHigher.Visible = False
optLower.Visible = False
cheatcounter = 0
End If
End If
If (total = -3) And (win = 0) Then
MsgBox "you're not very lucky", vbCritical, "Loser"
win = 1
ElseIf (total = -5) And (win = 0) Then
MsgBox "Give it up", vbCritical, "Loser"
```

```
win = 1
End If
End Sub
```

```
Private Sub optHigher_Click()
If counter = 1 Then
higher = 1
lower = 0
End If
End Sub
```

```
Private Sub optLower_Click()
If counter = 1 Then
higher = 0
lower = 1
End If
End Sub
```

```
Private Sub cmdExit_Click()
End
End Sub
```

```
Public Sub UserForm_Initialize()
cboLevel.AddItem "Easy"
cboLevel.AddItem "Medium"
cboLevel.AddItem "Hard"
End Sub
```

Code Listing 8.5 Higher/Lower game with difficulty levels

Much of the code is similar to our past projects. However, now along with adding the Public form load method for populating the new combo box, we use *if/then, else/if, else* to compare the names in the combo box. (Don't forget, when matching string data, letter case size must match.) The string variable called *level* holds the combo box choice. We assign the difficulty levels a number from one through ten, with ten being the hardest. This is accomplished by comparing the string variable to the combo box entries. If the user does not choose a level, a challenging level of nine is assigned to them by default. If the second random number generated is a winner, the *goto* cheat loop will pick another random number in the hopes that it will meet a condition in the code to cause a loss. The difficulty level determines the number of loops the *goto* instruction will cause to occur. Just as before, the bottom label displays score information, and annoying message boxes pop-up as the losses mount and the player scores negative points.

Chapter Eight Summary

Random numbers have many legitimate purposes in science and mathematics, but they can also be used for entertainment purposes. This chapter mainly focused on different manifestations of a higher/lower number game. Two different command buttons were coded to produce the numbers, and option buttons were used to select if the player believed the second number generated would be higher or lower in value. One button and a coded counter were also used. We are able to bring in the Windows Media Player for winning and losing sound effects. Odds were introduced by using a *goto* loop, which threw out a winning number and picked a different random number. We examined preset odds and various levels of difficulty adjusted by the user. The combo box was used, and the items were loaded into the box at run time using the Public function of form initialize. Labels were coded to change text during the program operation, and one label used the process of concatenation to display a message that included the player's score. Other more interesting and popular games will be examined next.

Chapter Nine

Traditional number games

Section 9.1. The Game of Twenty-one

The game of 21 (Blackjack) is a popular card game where players compete against the dealer for the highest score of 21 or below. Going above 21 is called a bust. The rules somewhat vary, but number cards are taken at their face value with picture cards (Jacks, Queen, and Kings) valued at 10 points. The Ace can be 11 points or 1 point at the player's discretion. Up to five cards are available, and the player automatically wins if they go up to five cards without going over 21. The dealer must take cards if they have under 17 points but cannot pull a card if they have over 16 points. If both player and dealer points match, then the dealer wins. Usually, if a player has two Aces, they have the option to split them into two separate hands. However, we will not include splitting Aces as part of our game. The Form shown in Figure 9.1 is for one person to play against an automated dealer. The default names are used for ten card labels on the form. Each has an associated label located to its side named *lblMyFirst* through *lblMyFifth*, and *lblDealFirst* through *lblDealFifth,* which are used to display the card values. As an additional project, you may wish to set the label property of visible to *false* for card labels three through five and have them appear as needed by using code such as "Label3.visible = *True*". The updated information labels under the numbers are named *lblMyTotal* and *lblDealTotal*. The buttons are named *cmdStart*, *cmdHit*, *cmdStay*, and *cmdExit*.

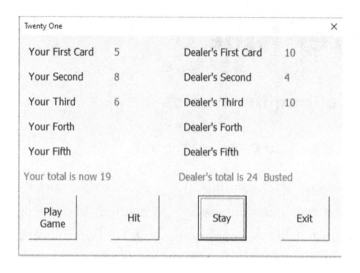

Figure 9.1 The game of 21

Some games use multiple decks of cards, and that is how our game is designed. Random numbers are generated between the values of two to ten points. Aces worth 11 points are also generated, but can be reduced to one point to not go over 21 and bust. The code uses public subroutines not linked to any object on the form. All lines of the public subroutines are typed in the code window, and it is standard practice to put them toward the bottom of the page. In Code listing 9.1, you will see that we use a public subroutine for clearing all variables and another for the player to set Aces' values through the use of an interactive message box.

```
Option Explicit
Dim myFirst As Integer
Dim mySecond As Integer
Dim myThird As Integer
Dim myForth As Integer
Dim myFifth As Integer
Dim myTotal As Integer
Dim dealFirst As Integer
Dim dealSecond As Integer
Dim dealThird As Integer
Dim dealForth As Integer
```

```vb
Dim dealFifth As Integer
Dim dealTotal As Integer
Dim hitCount As Integer
Dim yesNo As Integer
Dim acePick As Integer
Dim aceDealer3 As Boolean
Dim aceDealer4 As Boolean
Dim aceDealer5 As Boolean
Dim done As Boolean
```

```vb
Private Sub cmdStart_Click()
reset 'calls reset subroutine for game restart
Randomize Timer
myFirst = Int((Rnd * 10) + 2)
mySecond = Int((Rnd * 10) + 2)
myThird = Int((Rnd * 10) + 2)
myForth = Int((Rnd * 10) + 2)
myFifth = Int((Rnd * 10) + 2)
dealFirst = Int((Rnd * 10) + 2)
dealSecond = Int((Rnd * 10) + 2)
dealThird = Int((Rnd * 10) + 2)
dealForth = Int((Rnd * 10) + 2)
dealFifth = Int((Rnd * 10) + 2)

lblMyFirst = Str(myFirst)
If myFirst = 11 Then
ACE 'goes to ACE subroutine
myFirst = acePick
End If
lblMyFirst = Str(myFirst)

lblMySecond = Str(mySecond)
If mySecond = 11 Then
ACE 'goes to ACE subroutine
mySecond = acePick
End If
lblMySecond = Str(mySecond)
```

```
myTotal = myFirst + mySecond

lblDealFirst = Str(dealFirst)
lblDealSecond = Str(dealSecond)

If (dealFirst = 11) And (dealSecond = 11) Then
dealSecond = 1  'two Aces won't bust

End If

dealTotal = dealFirst + dealSecond
lblMyTotal = "Your total is " & (myTotal)
lblDealTotal = "Dealer's total is " & (dealTotal)
End Sub
```

```
Private Sub cmdHit_Click()
If (myTotal < 21) And (done = False) Then

Select Case hitCount
Case 0:
lblMyThird = myThird
If myThird = 11 Then
ACE 'goes to ACE subroutine
myThird = acePick
End If
lblMyThird = Str(myThird)
myTotal = myTotal + myThird
lblMyTotal = "Your total is now " & myTotal

Case 1:
lblMyForth = myForth
If myForth = 11 Then
ACE 'goes to ACE subroutine
myForth = acePick
End If
lblMyForth = Str(myForth)
myTotal = myTotal + myForth
```

```
lblMyTotal = "Your total is now " & myTotal


Case 2:
lblMyFifth = myFifth
If myFifth = 11 Then
ACE 'goes to ACE subroutine
myFifth = acePick
End If
lblMyFifth = Str(myFifth)
myTotal = myTotal + myFifth
lblMyTotal = "Your total is now " & myTotal


If myTotal < 22 Then
MsgBox "You Win with five cards", vbExclamation, "Winner"
reset 'calls subroutine
End If
End Select


hitCount = hitCount + 1


If myTotal > 21 Then
MsgBox "You're Busted", vbCritical, "You lose"
reset
End If


End If 'Ends top if statement
End Sub
```

```
Private Sub cmdStay_Click()
If (done = False) Then
If (dealTotal > 10) And (dealTotal < 17) And (dealThird = 11) Then
dealThird = 1      'So not busted by Ace
aceDealer3 = True
lblDealThird = "1"
dealTotal = dealTotal + 1
ElseIf (dealTotal < 17) And Not (aceDealer3 = True) Then
lblDealThird = Str(dealThird) 'dealer takes third
```

```
dealTotal = dealTotal + dealThird
End If                    'Third card done


If (dealTotal > 10) And (dealTotal < 17) And (dealForth = 11) Then
dealForth = 1  'Ace
aceDealer4 = True
lblDealForth = "1"
dealTotal = dealTotal + 1
ElseIf (dealTotal < 17) And Not (aceDealer4 = True) Then
lblDealForth = Str(dealForth) 'dealer takes forth
dealTotal = dealTotal + dealForth
End If                    'forth card done


If (dealTotal > 10) And (dealTotal < 17) And (dealFifth = 11) Then
dealFifth = 1   'Ace
aceDealer5 = True
lblDealFifth = "1"
dealTotal = dealTotal + 1
ElseIf (dealTotal < 17) And Not (aceDealer5 = True) Then
lblDealFifth = Str(dealFifth) 'dealer takes fifth
dealTotal = dealTotal + dealFifth
End If                    'Fifth card done


If (dealTotal > 21) Then
lblDealTotal = "Dealer's total is " & dealTotal & "  Busted"
done = True
ElseIf dealTotal < myTotal And Not (done = True) Then
lblMyTotal = "Player's total is " & myTotal & " Player Wins"
lblDealTotal = "Dealer's total is " & dealTotal
done = True
Else
lblDealTotal = "Dealer's total is " & dealTotal & "  Dealer Wins"
done = True 'doesn't allow for hit after game
End If   'Ends this section
End If    'Ends top If statement section
End Sub
```

```
Private Sub cmdExit_Click()
End
End Sub
```

```
Sub reset()
myFirst = 0
mySecond = 0
myThird = 0
myForth = 0
myFifth = 0
myTotal = 0
dealFirst = 0
dealSecond = 0
dealThird = 0
dealForth = 0
dealFifth = 0
dealTotal = 0
hitCount = 0
lblMyFirst = ""
lblMySecond = ""
lblMyThird = ""
lblMyForth = ""
lblMyFifth = ""
lblMyTotal = ""
lblDealFirst = ""
lblDealSecond = ""
lblDealThird = ""
lblDealForth = ""
lblDealFifth = ""
lblDealTotal = ""
acePick = 11
aceDealer3 = False
aceDealer4 = False
aceDealer5 = False
done = False
End Sub
```

```
Sub ACE()
yesNo = MsgBox("Do you want to keep as an Ace worth 11 points", vbYesNo, "ACE")
Select Case yesNo
Case 6:
acePick = 11
Case 7:
acePick = 1
End Select
End Sub
```

Code Listing 9.1 The Game of 21

The first line shows the *option explicit* command. It is a feature to help to remember to dimension variables as you add them to the code. It is helpful to enable this feature by choosing the *options* dropdown from the *tools* menu and checking the box to *require variable declaration*. There are many variables in the program because we use ten just to represent the playing cards. The first statement in the game start section calls the *reset* function to clear all variables and set the Boolean data types to *false* (False is equivalent to zero). All random numbers are then generated, and the first two cards for both player and dealer are displayed on the labels. If aces are generated for the player, the message box pops up to give the player the option of having the value either be 11 or 1. The dealer is also prevented in the code from having two Aces at 11 points each, causing a bust at the game's beginning. If that occurs, the second Ace changes to a one. All labels update after any changes. Also, in the Start section of the code, the player and dealer's first two card values are totaled and displayed on the associated information labels.

Both the *Hit* and *Stay* buttons contain an *If* condition, so that the buttons cannot be misused. The *Hit* code is entirely for the player. The variable *hitCount* is incremented towards the bottom of the subroutine each time the button is clicked. Since the number is incremented after the selection code, the value starts at zero. Using the *Select Case* conditions, the results for player cards three through five can be displayed. They are also each checked as being an Ace so the player can decide its value. Finally, if the player's total card value exceeds 21, the *bust* message is generated, and the game stops.

The *Stay* button switches activity to the dealer. Without intervention, the code picks each card, checks for Aces and changes the values accordingly, and then displays the dealer's final result compared to the player's score.

Just a few rules in any game cause the code to get quite expansive, but the fun of producing a game is worth the effort. I leave it up to you to develop a version of the program that can split player Aces or a version of the game that cheats. Our next project is a program for another popular Vegas-style game.

Section 9.2. The Dice Game of Craps

The game of Craps uses two dice pieces, and each is called a die. There are variations to the rules, but generally, the game has two sections. In the game's first section, the player rolls the dice and hopes for either a number 7 or 11 for an instant win. The player will lose on the first role if they roll a 2, 3, or 12, which is called crapping out. If the numbers 4, 5, 6, 8, 9, or 10 are the outcome of the first roll, then the number is called "the point," and the player will enter the second section of the game. The player will continue rolling the dice until they match the point and win, but they lose the game if number 7 comes up.

In our project, we must create pictures of six dice pieces, with dots showing the numbers one through six, as shown in Figure 9.2.

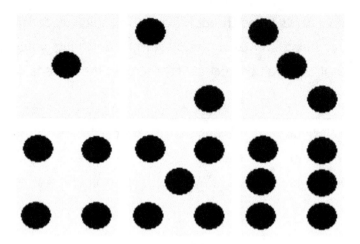

Figure 9.2 Pictures of dice

Each picture can be made using a photo program such as Paint. The picture size should match the image box size used on the form. We use a size of 100 for both height and width. Our background color for the dice pictures is yellow, but white is more traditional. The colors can be seen in the eBook version of the text. The form for the project appears in figure 9.3.

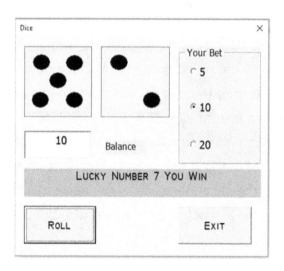

Figure 9.3 Dice game form

The default names of *image1* and *image2* are used, as is the *Balance* label's name. A frame was created, and the default name was kept, but the caption was changed to say "*Your Bet*" in 14-point font. The option buttons opt5, opt10, and opt20 were added inside the frame. Frames can be used to group options that can utilize arrays, but we are only using the frame for decoration on our form. The label above the command buttons is named *lblMessage,* and the caption for the label in the properties box states, "Place a bet and Roll the Bones." The message box will update as the game runs. Most of the code is in the *cmdRoll* command button routine, as shown in Code Listing 9.2.

```
Dim X As Integer
Dim Y As Integer
Dim z As Integer
Dim bet As Currency
Dim money As Currency
Dim roll As Integer
Dim numToHit As Integer
```

```
Private Sub cmdRoll_Click()
txtMoney.Text = Str(money)
lblMessage = ""
lblRollTheBones = ""
lblBalance = "Your Balance"

If roll = 0 Then 'start first secton

Randomize Timer
X = Int(Rnd * 5) + 1
Select Case X:
Case 1:
Image1.Picture = LoadPicture("C:\vb\dice1.bmp")
Case 2:
Image1.Picture = LoadPicture("C:\vb\dice2.bmp")
Case 3:
Image1.Picture = LoadPicture("C:\vb\dice3.bmp")
Case 4:
Image1.Picture = LoadPicture("C:\vb\dice4.bmp")
```

```
Case 5:
Image1.Picture = LoadPicture("C:\vb\dice5.bmp")
Case 6:
Image1.Picture = LoadPicture("C:\vb\dice6.bmp ")
End Select

Randomize Timer
Y = Int(Rnd * 5) + 1
Select Case Y
Case 1:
Image2.Picture = LoadPicture("C:\vb\dice1.bmp")
Case 2:
Image2.Picture = LoadPicture("C:\vb\dice2.bmp")
Case 3:
Image2.Picture = LoadPicture("C:\vb\dice3.bmp")
Case 4:
Image2.Picture = LoadPicture("C:\vb\dice4.bmp")
Case 5:
Image2.Picture = LoadPicture("C:\vb\dice5.bmp")
Case 6:
Image2.Picture = LoadPicture("C:\vb\dice6.bmp ")
End Select

z = X + Y 'total number for dice

'check first section results

If z = 2 Then
WindowsMediaPlayer1.URL = "C:\vb\chord.wav"
lblMessage = "Snake Eyes"
money = money - bet
txtMoney.Text = Str(money)
'MsgBox "Snake Eyes", vbExclamation, "Dice Game"
lblMessage = "Snake Eyes, Try it Again"
roll = 0

ElseIf z = 3 Then
```

```
WindowsMediaPlayer1.URL = "C:\vb\chord.wav"
money = money - bet
txtMoney.Text = Str(money)
'MsgBox "Craps, You Lose", vbExclamation, "Dice Game"
lblMessage = "Craps, Try Again"
roll = 0

ElseIf z = 12 Then
WindowsMediaPlayer1.URL = "C:\vb\chord.wav"
money = money - bet
txtMoney.Text = Str(money)
'MsgBox "Craps, You Lose", vbExclamation, "Dice Game"
lblMessage = "Try Again, go for 7 or 11"
roll = 0

'Winner code
ElseIf z = 7 Or z = 11 Then
WindowsMediaPlayer1.URL = "C:\vb\chimes.wav"
money = money + bet
txtMoney.Text = Str(money)
lblMessage = "Lucky Number " & (z) & " You Win"
roll = 0

Else
numToHit = z
WindowsMediaPlayer1.URL = "C:\vb\chimes.wav"
lblMessage = (z) & " is the point, roll another " & (z)
roll = 1

End If 'End first roll results

ElseIf roll = 1 Then 'Start second section 'And goneThrough = 1

Randomize Timer
X = Int(Rnd * 5) + 1
Select Case X:
Case 1:
```

```
Image1.Picture = LoadPicture("C:\dice game\dice1.bmp")
Case 2:
Image1.Picture = LoadPicture("C:\vb\dice2.bmp")
Case 3:
Image1.Picture = LoadPicture("C:\vb\dice3.bmp")
Case 4:
Image1.Picture = LoadPicture("C:\vb\dice4.bmp")
Case 5:
Image1.Picture = LoadPicture("C:\vb\dice5.bmp")
Case 6:
Image1.Picture = LoadPicture("C:\vb\dice6.bmp ")
End Select

Randomize Timer
Y = Int(Rnd * 5) + 1
Select Case Y
Case 1:
Image2.Picture = LoadPicture("C:\vb\dice1.bmp")
Case 2:
Image2.Picture = LoadPicture("C:\vb\dice2.bmp")
Case 3:
Image2.Picture = LoadPicture("C:\vb\dice3.bmp")
Case 4:
Image2.Picture = LoadPicture("C:\vb\dice4.bmp")
Case 5:
Image2.Picture = LoadPicture("C:\vb\dice5.bmp")
Case 6:
Image2.Picture = LoadPicture("C:\vb\dice6.bmp ")
End Select

z = X + Y 'total number for dice

'lose second section
If z = 7 Then
WindowsMediaPlayer1.URL = "C:\vb\chord.wav"
money = money - bet
txtMoney.Text = Str(money)
```

```
'MsgBox "7 You Lose", vbCritical, "Dice Game"
lblMessage = "Try Again, You Busted"
roll = 0
numToHit = 0

'win second section
ElseIf numToHit = z Then
WindowsMediaPlayer1.URL = "C:\vb\chord.wav"
money = money + bet
txtMoney.Text = Str(money)
'MsgBox "Winner", vbExclamation, "Dice Game"
lblMessage = "You Hit the Mark, number " & (z)
roll = 0
numToHit = 0

Else
lblMessage = (z) & " and you need " & (numToHit)
End If 'End second roll results
End If 'End secnd section
End Sub
```

```
Private Sub opt5_Click()
bet = 5
End Sub
```

```
Private Sub opt10_Click()
bet = 10
End Sub
```

```
Private Sub opt20_Click()
bet = 20
End Sub
```

```
Private Sub cmdExit_Click()
End
End Sub
```

Code Listing 9.2. Dice game program

Both sections of the game are coded in the roll button routine, but since the first section has the conditional code for the variable roll to be zero, it is executed at the beginning of the game. If the player wins or loses the first section, then the variable is reset to zero; otherwise, it is set to one. The *roll* variable will not send the procedure directly to the second section of the code because we are using an if/then else/if structure. After the first section executes, the subroutine is exited. The player not winning or losing directly in the first section will set up the variable to the number one, so that when the *roll* command button is clicked afterward, only the second section will run until a win or loss in that section will reset the *roll* variable. We are using the variables x for the first die and y for the second. It is a better procedure to be more descriptive in naming variables. We generate the random numbers and use the *select case* method to load the correct picture into the image box, but you could use if/then else/if statements if you wish. The code is reasonably well documented, and looking closely at the program. You should notice a comment apostrophe before the code for message box popups upon winning or losing. We say that they are "*commented out*". If you remove the apostrophe, the message boxes will be enabled. Having message boxes along with the on-screen messages of the label *lblMessage* seems a bit too much, but that is an individual taste. Some additional enhancements could be made for personal preferences. Earlier in the text, we presented code to eliminate number duplication, and you may wish to add that feature. Another issue that might be addressed is to lock out the bet option buttons once the roll is initiated, as it is now coded, the bet can be changed during the game.

All sounds and the six dice pictures must be in the vb folder on the C drive, or you can change the path in the code to reflect their location on your computer. The image *picture* property can be pointed to the pictures in the vb folder showing the dice at start-up. Having the two and the five showing will be a nice starting screen. You may also wish to adjust the property setting for color and font type and size, to make the form more appealing.

Chapter Nine Summary

Games with rules are possible to code and play with VBA. A game like Yahtzee, however, would take a large amount of coding. Blackjack and Craps require extensive coding but are doable since much of the code is redundant. We might attempt the game of Poker, but the pictures of the cards would be problematic, and the rules are more complex. We saw most decision-making is nicely handled by either the if/then, or if/then – else/if conditional statements. When there are many similar conditions in a row, it may be better to use the *select case* method. Creating nested conditional statements, such as we did in the last project, can seem a bit confusing at first glance, but It is an efficient way to drive code between different sections of the procedure. We saw again that lookup paths are extremely important and must be melodically laid out. It was also shown that in Visual Basic the object *properties* menu is very powerful. Next, we will produce a few custom games, and using the examples will help you to produce original games on new themes.

Chapter Ten

Custom games

Section 10.1. The Loan Shark Game

The next game is homemade and has six command buttons in play, requiring a lot of copying and pasting similar code sections having only minor changes. It is a game of chance where the player guesses which command button is the lucky number for the round. The game gives the player $100 to start, and the player has the option of betting 5, 10, or 20 dollars on their lucky number guesses. If the player runs out of money, they have the option of borrowing money from a loan shark. Eventually, the loan shark stops their credit and pays them a visit. The form is in Figure 10.1.

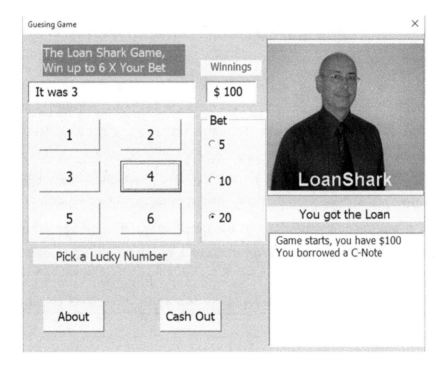

Figure 10.1 Loan Shark game

The command buttons are named cmd1 through cmd6 and use the caption property in the code to display *Winner* after a winning pick. It will change back to its number when next clicked. A frame labeled *Bet* contains the three option buttons, opt5, opt10, and opt20, which selects the bet amount of each round of play. Pictures are displayed in the *image1* box. The size dimensions of image1 on the form and the dimensions of the pictures must closely match. Images are loaded by code with the *loadPicture* statement specifying the path to the picture file. We again suggest using a folder named *vb* on the C drive to hold all images and sound files.

You can select an image while in the property window to load a happy picture at start-up. The code will load happy and sad pictures, and possibly a picture of the Loan shark, as the program runs its course. The Windows Media Player is placed on the form to produce sound, with its visible property set to False. The list box, located at the bottom right of the form, uses the default name, and messages from the Loan Shark appear in the box throughout the program by using the code's additem property. The name *lblMessage* refers to the label located just above the list box and is used to display messages as the program runs. Messages about the winning and losing numbers are displayed in the *txtMessage* text box, located just above the numbered command buttons. The label under the buttons is static and does not change, nor do the labels in the top left and center. Under the center label is a second text box named *txtMoney,* which displays the player's balance throughout the game. The command button labeled *About* is named *cmdAbout*, and displays the rules of the game in a message box. The button captioned *Cash Out* is named as cmdExit and ends the game. Most of the gameplay interactivity occurs as the numbered command buttons are clicked. The coding for the buttons is very similar and appears in Code Listing 10.1.

```
Dim X As Integer
Dim n As Integer
Dim Bet As Currency        'General Declarations Section
Dim SubTotal As Currency
```

```
Dim Game As Integer            'All that follows is code for #1 button:
Dim SharkMoney As Currency
Dim SharkCount As Integer
Dim Out As Integer
Dim Times As Integer
_____

Private Sub Cmd1_Click()
Select Case Game
Case 0: MsgBox "Place your Bet"        'message user forgot to bet

Case 1:
If SharkCount > 3 Then
Image1.Picture = LoadPicture("C:\dukish.jpg")
lblMessage = "You need to get the money"
 Out = MsgBox("The LoanShark is coming to visit you", vbCritical, "Out Of Luck")
 End
 End If


Loanshark = MsgBox("Want Money from the LoanShark?", vbYesNo, "Out of Money")
Image1.Picture = LoadPicture("C:\vb\dukish.jpg")
lblMessage = "You got the Loan"
 If Loanshark = 6 Then
 ListBox1.AddItem "You borrowed a C-Note"
 SharkMoney = SharkMoney + 100
 SharkCount = SharkCount + 1

 If SharkCount > 2 Then
 ListBox1.AddItem "You owe $" & Str(SharkMoney) & " and better pay it back!"
 End If

SubTotal = SubTotal + 100        'When user runs out of money, yes/no box pops up
txtMoney.Text = "$ " & SubTotal
Game = 2                 'Yes gives user a hundred dollars


Else
MsgBox "Game Over"
End                'No ends game
```

```
    End If

Case 2:                'If all is well, the game plays:
Randomize Timer
n = Int(Rnd * 6) + 1 'Produces a random number 1 to 6 for winning number

If 1 = n Then  'number picked

Randomize Timer
Times = Int(Rnd * 5) + 2 'Produces a random number 2 to 6 for times bet

txtMessage.Text = "Number " & n & " Winner" 'If random number matches button
Image1.Picture = LoadPicture("C:\vb\Happy.jpg")       'good things happen:
lblMessage = "You Won " & Times & " X Your Bet"     'Need to have files on C
WindowsMediaPlayer1.URL = "C:\vb\chimes.Wav" 'drive with matching names

SubTotal = SubTotal + Times * Bet
txtMoney.Text = "$ " & SubTotal
cmd1.Caption = "Winner"

Else

txtMessage.Text = "It was " & n         'If random number isn't a match
Image1.Picture = LoadPicture("C:\vb\Sad.jpg")      'bad things happen:
lblMessage = "You Lose"
WindowsMediaPlayer1.URL = "C:\vb\Chord.Wav"

SubTotal = SubTotal - Bet
txtMoney.Text = "$ " & SubTotal
cmd1.Caption = "1"
End If
End Select

If SubTotal <= 0 Then
Game = 1
End If
End Sub
```

```vb
Private Sub Cmd2_Click()
Select Case Game
Case 0: MsgBox "Place your Bet"        'message user forgot to bet

Case 1:
If SharkCount > 3 Then
Image1.Picture = LoadPicture("C:\vb\dukish.jpg")
lblMessage = "You got the Loan"
Out = MsgBox("The LoanShark is coming to visit you", vbCritical, "Out Of Luck")
End
End If

Loanshark = MsgBox("Want Money from the LoanShark?", vbYesNo, "Out of Money")
Image1.Picture = LoadPicture("C:\vb\dukish.jpg")
lblMessage = "You got the Loan"
If Loanshark = 6 Then
ListBox1.AddItem "You borrowed a C-Note"
SharkMoney = SharkMoney + 100
SharkCount = SharkCount + 1

If SharkCount > 2 Then
ListBox1.AddItem "You owe $" & Str(SharkMoney) & " and better pay it back!"
End If

SubTotal = SubTotal + 100        'When user runs out of money, yes/no box pops up
txtMoney.Text = "$ " & SubTotal
Game = 2                'Yes gives user a hundred dollars

Else
MsgBox "Game Over"
End                'No ends game
End If

Case 2:                'If all is well, the game plays:
Randomize Timer
n = Int(Rnd * 6) + 1 'Produces a random number 1 to 6 for winning number
```

```
If 2 = n Then 'number picked

Randomize Timer
Times = Int(Rnd * 5) + 2 'Produces a random number 2 to 6 for times bet


txtMessage.Text = "Yes, number " & n & " Winner"  'If random number matches button
Image1.Picture = LoadPicture("C:\vb\Happy.jpg")      'good things happen:
lblMessage = "You Won " & Times & " X Your Bet"
WindowsMediaPlayer1.URL = "C:\vb\chimes.Wav

SubTotal = SubTotal + Times * Bet
txtMoney.Text = "$ " & SubTotal
cmd2.Caption = "Winner"

Else

txtMessage.Text = "It was " & n        'If random number isn't a match
Image1.Picture = LoadPicture("C:\vb\Sad.jpg")     'bad things happen:
lblMessage = "You Lose"
WindowsMediaPlayer1.URL = "C:\vb\Chord.Wav"

SubTotal = SubTotal - Bet
txtMoney.Text = "$ " & SubTotal
cmd2.Caption = "2"
End If
End Select

If SubTotal <= 0 Then
Game = 1
End If
End Sub
```

```
Private Sub Cmd3_Click()
Select Case Game
```

```
Case 0: MsgBox "Place your Bet"          'message user forgot to bet

Case 1:
If SharkCount > 3 Then
Image1.Picture = LoadPicture("C:\vb\dukish.jpg")
lblMessage = "You got the Loan"
 Out = MsgBox("The LoanShark is coming to visit you", vbCritical, "Out Of Luck")
 End
 End If

Loanshark = MsgBox("Want Money from the LoanShark?", vbYesNo, "Out of Money")
Image1.Picture = LoadPicture("C:\vb\dukish.jpg")
 lblMessage = "You got the Loan"
If Loanshark = 6 Then
ListBox1.AddItem "You borrowed a C-Note"
SharkMoney = SharkMoney + 100
SharkCount = SharkCount + 1

If SharkCount > 2 Then
ListBox1.AddItem "You owe $" & Str(SharkMoney) & " and better pay it back!"
End If

SubTotal = SubTotal + 100      'When user runs out of money, yes/no box pops up
txtMoney.Text = "$ " & SubTotal
Game = 2                'Yes gives user a hundred dollars

Else
MsgBox "Game Over"
End                'No ends game
End If

Case 2:                'If all is well, the game plays:
Randomize Timer
n = Int(Rnd * 6) + 1 'Produces a random number 1 to 6for winning number

If 3 = n Then 'The number was picked
```

```
Randomize Timer
Times = Int(Rnd * 5) + 2 'Produces a random number 2 to 6 for times bet

If 2 > Times Then
Times = 2 ' assures bet gets at least doubled
End If

txtMessage.Text = "Number " & n & " Winner"  'If random number matches button
number
Image1.Picture = LoadPicture("C:\vb\Happy.jpg")      'good things happen:
lblMessage = "You Got Back " & Times & " X Your Bet"
WindowsMediaPlayer1.URL = "C:\vb\chimes.Wav"

SubTotal = SubTotal + Times * Bet
txtMoney.Text = "$ " & SubTotal
cmd3.Caption = "Winner"

Else

txtMessage.Text = "It was " & n          'If random number isn't a match
Image1.Picture = LoadPicture("C:\vb\Sad.jpg")      'bad things happen:
lblMessage = "You Lose"
WindowsMediaPlayer1.URL = "C:\vb\Chord.Wav"

SubTotal = SubTotal - Bet
txtMoney.Text = "$ " & SubTotal
cmd3.Caption = "3"
End If
End Select

If SubTotal <= 0 Then
Game = 1
End If
End Sub
```

```
Private Sub Cmd4_Click()
Select Case Game
```

```
Case 0: MsgBox "Place your Bet"         'message user forgot to bet


Case 1:
If SharkCount > 3 Then
Image1.Picture = LoadPicture("C:\vb\dukish.jpg")
lblMessage = "You got the Loan"
 Out = MsgBox("The LoanShark is coming to visit you", vbCritical, "Out Of Luck")
 End
 End If


Loanshark = MsgBox("Want Money from the LoanShark?", vbYesNo, "Out of Money")
Image1.Picture = LoadPicture("C:\vb\dukish.jpg")
lblMessage = "You got the Loan"
 If Loanshark = 6 Then
 ListBox1.AddItem "You borrowed a C-Note"
 SharkMoney = SharkMoney + 100
 SharkCount = SharkCount + 1

 If SharkCount > 2 Then
 ListBox1.AddItem "You owe $" & Str(SharkMoney) & " and better pay it back!"
 End If


 SubTotal = SubTotal + 100        'When user runs out of money, yes/no box pops up
 txtMoney.Text = "$ " & SubTotal
 Game = 2                'Yes gives user a hundred dollars


 Else
 MsgBox "Game Over"
 End                'No ends game
 End If

Case 2:                'If all is well, the game plays:
Randomize Timer
n = Int(Rnd * 6) + 1 'Produces a random number 1 to 6 for winning number

If 4 = n Then  'number picked
```

```
Randomize Timer
Times = Int(Rnd * 5) + 2 'Produces a random number 2 to 6 for times bet

txtMessage.Text = n & " is a Winner"  'If random number matches button number
Image1.Picture = LoadPicture("C:\vb\Happy.jpg")      'good things happen:
lblMessage = "Winner of " & Times & " X Your Bet"
WindowsMediaPlayer1.URL = "C:\vb\chimes.Wav"

SubTotal = SubTotal + Times * Bet
txtMoney.Text = "$ " & SubTotal
cmd4.Caption = "Winner"

Else

txtMessage.Text = "It was " & n       'If random number isn't a match
Image1.Picture = LoadPicture("C:\vb\Sad.jpg")     'bad things happen:
lblMessage = "You Lose"
WindowsMediaPlayer1.URL = "C:\vb\Chord.Wav"

SubTotal = SubTotal - Bet
txtMoney.Text = "$ " & SubTotal
cmd4.Caption = "4"
End If
End Select

If SubTotal <= 0 Then
Game = 1
End If
End Sub
_____

Private Sub Cmd5_Click()
Select Case Game
Case 0: MsgBox "Place your Bet"        'message user forgot to bet

Case 1:
If SharkCount > 3 Then
```

```
Image1.Picture = LoadPicture("C:\vb\dukish.jpg")
lblMessage = "You got the Loan"
 Out = MsgBox("The LoanShark is coming to visit you", vbCritical, "Out Of Luck")
 End
 End If


Loanshark = MsgBox("Want Money from the LoanShark?", vbYesNo, "Out of Money")
Image1.Picture = LoadPicture("C:\vb\dukish.jpg")
 lblMessage = "You got the Loan"
 If Loanshark = 6 Then
ListBox1.AddItem "You borrowed a C-Note"
SharkMoney = SharkMoney + 100
SharkCount = SharkCount + 1

If SharkCount > 2 Then
ListBox1.AddItem "You owe $" & Str(SharkMoney) & " and better pay it back!"
End If


SubTotal = SubTotal + 100      'When user runs out of money, yes/no box pops up
txtMoney.Text = "$ " & SubTotal
Game = 2              'Yes gives user a hundred dollars


Else
MsgBox "Game Over"
End                'No ends game
End If


Case 2:             'If all is well, the game plays:
Randomize Timer
n = Int(Rnd * 6) + 1 'Produces a random number 1 to 6 for winning number

If 5 = n Then  'number picked

Randomize Timer
Times = Int(Rnd * 5) + 2 'Produces a random number 2 to 6 for times bet

txtMessage.Text = "Yes " & n & " is a Winner"  'If random number matches button
```

```vb
Image1.Picture = LoadPicture("C:\vb\Happy.jpg")        'good things happen:
lblMessage = "Winner of " & Times & " X Your Bet"
WindowsMediaPlayer1.URL = "C:\vb\chimes.Wav"

SubTotal = SubTotal + Times * Bet
txtMoney.Text = "$ " & SubTotal
cmd5.Caption = "Winner"

Else

txtMessage.Text = "It was " & n          'If random number isn't a match
Image1.Picture = LoadPicture("C:\vb\Sad.jpg")      'bad things happen:
lblMessage = "You Lose"
WindowsMediaPlayer1.URL = "C:\vb\Chord.Wav"

SubTotal = SubTotal - Bet
txtMoney.Text = "$ " & SubTotal
cmd5.Caption = "5"
End If
End Select

If SubTotal <= 0 Then
Game = 1
End If
End Sub
```

```vb
Private Sub Cmd6_Click()
Select Case Game
Case 0: MsgBox "Place your Bet"        'message user forgot to bet

Case 1:
If SharkCount > 3 Then
Image1.Picture = LoadPicture("C:\vb\dukish.jpg")
lblMessage = "You got the Loan"
 Out = MsgBox("The LoanShark is coming to visit you", vbCritical, "Out Of Luck")
 End
 End If
```

```
Loanshark = MsgBox("Want Money from the LoanShark?", vbYesNo, "Out of Money")
Image1.Picture = LoadPicture("C:\vb\dukish.jpg")
lblMessage = "You got the Loan"
 If Loanshark = 6 Then
ListBox1.AddItem "You borrowed a C-Note"
SharkMoney = SharkMoney + 100
SharkCount = SharkCount + 1

If SharkCount > 2 Then
ListBox1.AddItem "You owe $" & Str(SharkMoney) & " and better pay it back!"
End If

SubTotal = SubTotal + 100        'When user runs out of money, yes/no box pops up
txtMoney.Text = "$ " & SubTotal
Game = 2                'Yes gives user a hundred dollars

Else
MsgBox "Game Over"
End                'No ends game
End If

Case 2:                'If all is well, the game plays:
Randomize Timer
n = Int(Rnd * 6) + 1 'Produces a random number 1 to 6 for winning number

If 6 = n Then  'number picked

Randomize Timer
Times = Int(Rnd * 5) + 2 'Produces a random number 2 to 6 for times bet

txtMessage.Text = "Yes " & n & " is a Winner" 'If random number matches button
Image1.Picture = LoadPicture("C:\vb\Happy.jpg")      'good things happen:
lblMessage = "Winner of " & Times & " X Your Bet"
WindowsMediaPlayer1.URL = "C:\vb\chimes.Wav"

SubTotal = SubTotal + Times * Bet
```

```vb
txtMessage.Text = "$ " & SubTotal
cmd6.Caption = "Winner"

Else

txtMessage.Text = "It was " & n        'If random number isn't a match
Image1.Picture = LoadPicture("C:\vb\Sad.jpg")     'bad things happen:
lblMessage = "You Lose"
WindowsMediaPlayer1.URL = "C:\vb\Chord.Wav"

SubTotal = SubTotal - Bet
txtMoney.Text = "$ " & SubTotal
cmd6.Caption = "6"
End If
End Select

If SubTotal <= 0 Then
Game = 1
End If
End Sub
```

```vb
Private Sub Opt5_Click()
Bet = 5                 'allows game to play
Game = 2
End Sub
```

```vb
Private Sub Opt10_Click()
Bet = 10                 'allows game to play
Game = 2
End Sub
```

```vb
Private Sub Opt20_Click()
Bet = 20                 'allows game to play
Game = 2
End Sub
```

```vb
Private Sub cmdAbout_Click()
```

```vba
MsgBox "The game starts with $100, and you can borrow money from a Loanshark. You
can win up to 6 times your bet."
End Sub
```

```vba
Private Sub CmdExit_Click()
MsgBox "Your Cash Out is $" & SubTotal
End
End Sub
```

```vba
Private Sub UserForm_Initialize()
txtMessage.Text = "Place your Bet, to Win."
SubTotal = 100
txtMoney.Text = "$ " & SubTotal          'Shows the $100 in the textbox
ListBox1.AddItem "Game starts, you have $100"
End Sub
```
Code Listing 10.1 Loan Shark game

The *UserForm_Initialize* subroutine can be modified by double-clicking on the form and changing it as is shown in the listing, or it can be added manually. Because Visual Basic is object-oriented, the location of the subroutines as part of the overall code is inconsequential. Still, it is tidy to have functions and basic subroutines located towards the bottom of the code. It is somewhat confusing in VBA that the method is called *Initialize,* whereas, in regular VB, the method is called *Form Load.* As the form loads and the program begins, the balance variable called *SubTotal* starts with a value of 100. It is declared as a currency data type in the code's general declarations section, but we use the convert to a string function *CStr()* before display. The Currency data type will usually display the value as dollars and cents, and you may wish to experiment with displaying it in that way.

For the command button code, we see the use of the *Select Case* decision for the integer variable named Game. The zero case occurs when the command button is clicked, but no option button was selected to determine a bet amount. Each option button sets the *Game* variable to the value of two. Case two will run if all is well, with the player above a zero or negative balance. A random number is generated, and if it matches the button number, then a multiplication amount called *Times* of between two and six is determined. Happy sounds, images, and messages are displayed, and the player's balance called *SubTotal* is incremented by the option button's *Bet* variable multiplied by the random number multiplier, which is called *Times*. This process occurs with the formula in the code: SubTotal = SubTotal + Times * Bet. (The asterisk is the character used to denote multiplication.)

If there was not a match between the random lucky number and the numbered command button which the user clicked, then the *SubTotal* amount will be decremented by the bet amount. In that case, bad sounds, images, and messages will occur, and if the subtotal is at zero or below, then the *Game* variable, used for the *Select Case* condition, will be changed to a value of one, which then selects the Loan Shark code.

A counter called *SharkCount* determines the response during Game condition one. The player is given the option through an interactive message box to accept a load from the Loan Shark. A negative response from the player will end the game. If the player accepts a loan, the amount is listed using the *addItem* method into the list box, and play will resume. By examining the SharkCounter value, which increments on each loan transaction, various sounds and messages occur as money is borrowed from the Loan Shark. The game terminates when the *SharkCount* variable becomes greater than three, and the game ends with an ominous message.

Section 10.2. The memory Game

The game uses random numbers to generate eight color pictures on the form in which the player blackens out and proceeds to identify color matching locations to score points. It is a game that is relativity difficult for me since I have a terrible memory. It could be quite useful as a tool to improve memory and can easily be adapted to help people of both a younger and older age improve cognitive skills and memory. The project's form originally was less cluttered, with the player able to simply click the pictures in order to match colors and score points; however, newer VBA editions have updated the image object not to use the click method, so the form now presented in Figure 10.2 has command buttons for the user to click when selecting the associated image.

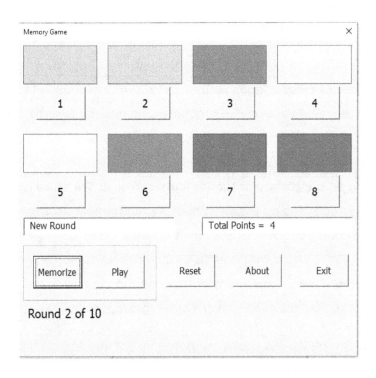

Figure 10.2 Memory game

The image sizes in the form shown are 100 pixels wide by 50 high and named picture1 one through picture8. You must set their image properties to enabled as *False*; otherwise, the program will not work correctly if a user happens to click an image. The associated command buttons are named cmd1 through cmd8. The text box where the text New Round is showing in the diagram is named Text1, and the text box to the right is named Text2.

The names of the command buttons below are: cmdMemorize, cmdPlay, cmdReset, cmdAbout, and cmdExit. The frame placed around the *memorize* and *play* buttons helps the user identify the most useful buttons but is unnecessary. If you use the frame, it must be placed on the form first with the buttons then added inside of the frame. In Figure 10.2, the bottom text is a label that changes with the code and has the name Label1 by default. In the caption property window, we added the following information to be displayed at start-up: *1. Memorize, 2. Play, 3. Match number to Win.* The label then goes on to display updated information as the game progresses.

The first step of play is to click the memorize button, which displays a random pattern of color images so that there are two of each of the colors: red, green, blue, and yellow. The second step is for the user to click the play button, which hides all color images by displaying a black picture over them. Since the image only consists of a solid color, the size is not much of an issue, as long as the picture is slightly larger in size. We store all color pictures and sound files on the C drive in the vb folder with the file names as shown in the code path. As the player matches each of the two color images, the score for the round increments, and the total score accumulates. After each round, the player clicks memorize again and continues the process until ten rounds have elapsed. The player is then prompted to reset the game.

Additionally, the player can reset the game at any time to clear all round and the total score tally. The *About* button brings up a message box displaying the rules of the game. The code is very repetitive, as in the last project, where the image section is very similar, with minor variations only needed for each specific image, and there is much copying and pasting used in the code appearing in Code Listing 10.2. We have not added any safeguards where the colors must be hidden during gameplay, and if the player fails to click the play button, they can cheat by seeing the colors and simply clicking on them. You may wish to add code to safeguard against this issue.

```
Dim cardOne As Integer
```

```
Dim cardTwo As Integer
Dim cardThree As Integer
Dim cardFour As Integer
Dim cardFive As Integer
Dim cardSix As Integer
Dim cardSeven As Integer
Dim cardEight As Integer
Dim counter As Integer
Dim matches As Integer
Dim color As Integer
Dim red As Integer
Dim green As Integer
Dim blue As Integer
Dim yellow As Integer
Dim x As String
Dim y As Integer
Dim Pic1 As Integer
Dim Pic2 As Integer
Dim Pic3 As Integer
Dim Pic4 As Integer
Dim Pic5 As Integer
Dim Pic6 As Integer
Dim Pic7 As Integer
Dim Pic8 As Integer
Dim cardOneSelect As Integer
Dim cardTwoSelect As Integer
Dim cardThreeSelect As Integer
Dim cardFourSelect As Integer
Dim cardFiveSelect As Integer
Dim cardSixSelect As Integer
Dim cardSevenSelect As Integer
Dim cardEightSelect As Integer
Dim cardOnePickedColor As Integer
Dim cardTwoPickedColor As Integer
Dim cardThreePickedColor As Integer
Dim cardFourPickedColor As Integer
Dim cardFivePickedColor As Integer
```

```
Dim cardSixPickedColor As Integer
Dim cardSevenPickedColor As Integer
Dim cardEightPickedColor As Integer
Dim GameCounter As Integer
Dim totalMatches As Integer
Dim totalPoints As Integer
Dim roundPoints As Integer
```

```
Private Sub cmdAbout_Click()
MsgBox "Click memorize, then Hide and match the squares. After 10 rounds, Reset starts
a new game", vbInformation, "Memory Game Help"
End Sub
```

```
Private Sub cmdMemorize_Click()  'generate random numbers assign colors
GameCounter = GameCounter + 1
red = 0
green = 0
blue = 0
yellow = 0
cardOne = 0
cardTwo = 0
cardThree = 0
cardFour = 0
cardFive = 0
cardSix = 0
cardSeven = 0
cardEight = 0
cardOneSelect = 0
cardTwoSelect = 0
cardThreeSelect = 0
cardFourSelect = 0
cardFiveSelect = 0
cardSixSelect = 0
cardSevenSelect = 0
cardEightSelect = 0
cmd1.Caption = "1"
cmd2.Caption = "2"
```

```
cmd3.Caption = "3"
cmd4.Caption = "4"
cmd5.Caption = "5"
cmd6.Caption = "6"
cmd7.Caption = "7"
cmd8.Caption = "8"

If GameCounter > 10 Then
Label1 = "Reset for New Game"
WindowsMediaPlayer1.URL = "C:\vb\chimes.wav"
Else
roundPoints = roundPoints + matches
matches = 0                    'display information
counter = 0
Text1.Text = "New Round"
Label1 = "Round " & GameCounter & " of 10"

Do Until red = 2 And green = 2 And blue = 2 And yellow = 2

Randomize Timer              'loop until two of each color cards are picked
cardOne = Int(Rnd * 4)
cardTwo = Int(Rnd * 4)
cardThree = Int(Rnd * 4)
cardFour = Int(Rnd * 4)
cardFive = Int(Rnd * 4)
cardSix = Int(Rnd * 4)
cardSeven = Int(Rnd * 4)
cardEight = Int(Rnd * 4)

If cardOneSelect < 1 And cardOne = 0 And red < 2 Then
Pic1 = 1                  'Determines card
red = red + 1               'Allows only two color cards to appear
cardOneSelect = 1                'locks out card
cardOnePickedColor = cardOne       'sends color information to specific card
ElseIf cardOneSelect < 1 And cardOne = 1 And green < 2 Then
Pic1 = 2
green = green + 1
```

```
cardOneSelect = 1
cardOnePickedColor = cardOne
ElseIf cardOneSelect < 1 And cardOne = 2 And blue < 2 Then
Pic1 = 3
blue = blue + 1
cardOneSelect = 1
cardOnePickedColor = cardOne
ElseIf cardOneSelect < 1 And cardOne = 3 And yellow < 2 Then
Pic1 = 4
yellow = yellow + 1
cardOneSelect = 1
cardOnePickedColor = cardOne
Else: y = 1
End If


If cardTwoSelect < 1 And cardTwo = 0 And red < 2 Then
Pic2 = 1
red = red + 1
cardTwoSelect = 1
cardTwoPickedColor = cardTwo
ElseIf cardTwoSelect < 1 And cardTwo = 1 And green < 2 Then
Pic2 = 2
green = green + 1
cardTwoSelect = 1
cardTwoPickedColor = cardTwo
ElseIf cardTwoSelect < 1 And cardTwo = 2 And blue < 2 Then
Pic2 = 3
blue = blue + 1
cardTwoSelect = 1
cardTwoPickedColor = cardTwo
ElseIf cardTwoSelect < 1 And cardTwo = 3 And yellow < 2 Then
Pic2 = 4
yellow = yellow + 1
cardTwoSelect = 1
cardTwoPickedColor = cardTwo
Else: y = 1
End If
```

```
If cardThreeSelect < 1 And cardThree = 0 And red < 2 Then
Pic3 = 1
red = red + 1
cardThreeSelect = 1
cardThreePickedColor = cardThree
ElseIf cardThreeSelect < 1 And cardThree = 1 And green < 2 Then
Pic3 = 2
green = green + 1
cardThreeSelect = 1
cardThreePickedColor = cardThree
ElseIf cardThreeSelect < 1 And cardThree = 2 And blue < 2 Then
Pic3 = 3
blue = blue + 1
cardThreeSelect = 1
cardThreePickedColor = cardThree
ElseIf cardThreeSelect < 1 And cardThree = 3 And yellow < 2 Then
Pic3 = 4
yellow = yellow + 1
cardThreeSelect = 1
cardThreePickedColor = cardThree
Else: y = 1
End If

If cardFourSelect < 1 And cardFour = 0 And red < 2 Then
Pic4 = 1
red = red + 1
cardFourSelect = 1
cardFourPickedColor = cardFour
ElseIf cardFourSelect < 1 And cardFour = 1 And green < 2 Then
Pic4 = 2
green = green + 1
cardFourSelect = 1
cardFourPickedColor = cardFour
ElseIf cardFourSelect < 1 And cardFour = 2 And blue < 2 Then
Pic4 = 3
blue = blue + 1
```

```
cardFourSelect = 1
cardFourPickedColor = cardFour
ElseIf cardFourSelect < 1 And cardFour = 3 And yellow < 2 Then
Pic4 = 4
yellow = yellow + 1
cardFourSelect = 1
cardFourPickedColor = cardFour
Else: y = 1
End If

If cardFiveSelect < 1 And cardFive = 0 And red < 2 Then
Pic5 = 1
red = red + 1
cardFiveSelect = 1
cardFivePickedColor = cardFive
ElseIf cardFiveSelect < 1 And cardFive = 1 And green < 2 Then
Pic5 = 2
green = green + 1
cardFiveSelect = 1
cardFivePickedColor = cardFive
ElseIf cardFiveSelect < 1 And cardFive = 2 And blue < 2 Then
Pic5 = 3
blue = blue + 1
cardFiveSelect = 1
cardFivePickedColor = cardFive
ElseIf cardFiveSelect < 1 And cardFive = 3 And yellow < 2 Then
Pic5 = 4
yellow = yellow + 1
cardFiveSelect = 1
cardFivePickedColor = cardFive
Else: y = 1
End If

If cardSixSelect < 1 And cardSix = 0 And red < 2 Then
Pic6 = 1
red = red + 1
cardSixSelect = 1
```

```
cardSixPickedColor = cardSix
ElseIf cardSixSelect < 1 And cardSix = 1 And green < 2 Then
Pic6 = 2
green = green + 1
cardSixSelect = 1
cardSixPickedColor = cardSix
ElseIf cardSixSelect < 1 And cardSix = 2 And blue < 2 Then
Pic6 = 3
blue = blue + 1
cardSixSelect = 1
cardSixPickedColor = cardSix
ElseIf cardSixSelect < 1 And cardSix = 3 And yellow < 2 Then
Pic6 = 4
yellow = yellow + 1
cardSixSelect = 1
cardSixPickedColor = cardSix
Else: y = 1
End If

If cardSevenSelect < 1 And cardSeven = 0 And red < 2 Then
Pic7 = 1
red = red + 1
cardSevenSelect = 1
cardSevenPickedColor = cardSeven
ElseIf cardSevenSelect < 1 And cardSeven = 1 And green < 2 Then
Pic7 = 2
green = green + 1
cardSevenSelect = 1
cardSevenPickedColor = cardSeven
ElseIf cardSevenSelect < 1 And cardSeven = 2 And blue < 2 Then
Pic7 = 3
blue = blue + 1
cardSevenSelect = 1
cardSevenPickedColor = cardSeven
ElseIf cardSevenSelect < 1 And cardSeven = 3 And yellow < 2 Then
Pic7 = 4
yellow = yellow + 1
```

```
cardSevenSelect = 1
cardSevenPickedColor = cardSeven
Else: y = 1
End If


If cardEightSelect < 1 And cardEight = 0 And red < 2 Then
Pic8 = 1
red = red + 1
cardEightSelect = 1
cardEightPickedColor = cardEight
ElseIf cardEightSelect < 1 And cardEight = 1 And green < 2 Then
Pic8 = 2
green = green + 1
cardEightSelect = 1
cardEightPickedColor = cardEight
ElseIf cardEightSelect < 1 And cardEight = 2 And blue < 2 Then
Pic8 = 3
blue = blue + 1
cardEightSelect = 1
cardEightPickedColor = cardEight
ElseIf cardEightSelect < 1 And cardEight = 3 And yellow < 2 Then
Pic8 = 4
yellow = yellow + 1
cardEightSelect = 1
cardEightPickedColor = cardEight
Else: y = 1
End If


Loop     'End of color card pick do--until loop

Select Case Pic1              'Turns color information to color picture
Case 1
picture1.Picture = LoadPicture("C:\vb\red.bmp")
Case 2
picture1.Picture = LoadPicture("C:\vb\green.bmp")
Case 3
picture1.Picture = LoadPicture("C:\vb\blue.bmp")
```

```
Case 4
picture1.Picture = LoadPicture("C:\vb\yellow.bmp")
End Select

Select Case Pic2
Case 1
picture2.Picture = LoadPicture("C:\vb\red.bmp")
Case 2
picture2.Picture = LoadPicture("C:\vb\green.bmp")
Case 3
picture2.Picture = LoadPicture("C:\vb\blue.bmp")
Case 4
picture2.Picture = LoadPicture("C:\vb\yellow.bmp")
End Select

Select Case Pic3
Case 1
picture3.Picture = LoadPicture("C:\vb\red.bmp")
Case 2
picture3.Picture = LoadPicture("C:\vb\green.bmp")
Case 3
picture3.Picture = LoadPicture("C:\vb\blue.bmp")
Case 4
picture3.Picture = LoadPicture("C:\vb\yellow.bmp")
End Select

Select Case Pic4
Case 1
picture4.Picture = LoadPicture("C:\vb\red.bmp")
Case 2
picture4.Picture = LoadPicture("C:\vb\green.bmp")
Case 3
picture4.Picture = LoadPicture("C:\vb\blue.bmp")
Case 4
picture4.Picture = LoadPicture("C:\vb\yellow.bmp")
End Select
```

```
Select Case Pic5
Case 1
picture5.Picture = LoadPicture("C:\vb\red.bmp")
Case 2
picture5.Picture = LoadPicture("C:\vb\green.bmp")
Case 3
picture5.Picture = LoadPicture("C:\vb\blue.bmp")
Case 4
picture5.Picture = LoadPicture("C:\vb\yellow.bmp")
End Select

Select Case Pic6
Case 1
picture6.Picture = LoadPicture("C:\vb\red.bmp")
Case 2
picture6.Picture = LoadPicture("C:\vb\green.bmp")
Case 3
picture6.Picture = LoadPicture("C:\vb\blue.bmp")
Case 4
picture6.Picture = LoadPicture("C:\vb\yellow.bmp")
End Select

Select Case Pic7
Case 1
picture7.Picture = LoadPicture("C:\vb\red.bmp")
Case 2
picture7.Picture = LoadPicture("C:\vb\green.bmp")
Case 3
picture7.Picture = LoadPicture("C:\vb\blue.bmp")
Case 4
picture7.Picture = LoadPicture("C:\vb\yellow.bmp")
End Select

Select Case Pic8
Case 1
picture8.Picture = LoadPicture("C:\vb\red.bmp")
Case 2
```

```
picture8.Picture = LoadPicture("C:\vb\green.bmp")
Case 3
picture8.Picture = LoadPicture("C:\vb\blue.bmp")
Case 4
picture8.Picture = LoadPicture("C:\vb\yellow.bmp")
End Select
End If
End Sub
```

```
Private Sub cmdPlay_Click()      'hide colors and zero counter
picture1.Picture = LoadPicture("C:\vb\black.bmp")
picture2.Picture = LoadPicture("C:\vb\black.bmp")
picture3.Picture = LoadPicture("C:\vb\black.bmp")
picture4.Picture = LoadPicture("C:\vb\black.bmp")
picture5.Picture = LoadPicture("C:\vb\black.bmp")
picture6.Picture = LoadPicture("C:\vb\black.bmp")
picture7.Picture = LoadPicture("C:\vb\black.bmp")
picture8.Picture = LoadPicture("C:\vb\black.bmp")

Text1 = "Points = " & Str(matches)
counter = 0
End Sub
```

```
Private Sub cmd1_Click()
'Checks for first click and picks color to match

If counter = 0 And cardOnePickedColor < 10 Then
color = cardOnePickedColor

Select Case cardOnePickedColor
Case 0
picture1.Picture = LoadPicture("C:\vb\red.bmp")
x = "RED"
Case 1
picture1.Picture = LoadPicture("C:\vb\green.bmp")
x = "GREEN"
Case 2
```

```
picture1.Picture = LoadPicture("C:\vb\blue.bmp")
x = "BLUE"
Case 3
picture1.Picture = LoadPicture("C:\vb\yellow.bmp")
x = "Yellow"
End Select

Label1 = "Looking for " & (x)
cmd1.Caption = "Picked"
counter = counter + 1

Else                            'Checks for a winning match
WindowsMediaPlayer1.URL = "C:\vb\chimes.wav"
cmd1.Caption = "Picked"
If color = cardOnePickedColor Then
Select Case cardOnePickedColor
Case 0
picture1.Picture = LoadPicture("C:\vb\red.bmp")
Case 1
picture1.Picture = LoadPicture("C:\vb\green.bmp")
Case 2
picture1.Picture = LoadPicture("C:\vb\blue.bmp")
Case 3
picture1.Picture = LoadPicture("C:\vb\yellow.bmp")
End Select

matches = matches + 1
Text1 = "Points = " & Str(matches)
totalPoints = roundPoints + matches
Text2 = "Total Points = " & Str(totalPoints)
Label1 = "Got It"
counter = 0

Else: WindowsMediaPlayer1.URL = "C:\vb\chord.wav"      'no match loses
Select Case cardOnePickedColor
Case 0
picture1.Picture = LoadPicture("C:\vb\red.bmp")
```

```vb
Case 1
picture1.Picture = LoadPicture("C:\vb\green.bmp")
Case 2
picture1.Picture = LoadPicture("C:\vb\blue.bmp")
Case 3
picture1.Picture = LoadPicture("C:\vb\yellow.bmp")
End Select
End If
End If
cardOnePickedColor = 10   'lockout setting the card to 10
End Sub
```

```vb
Private Sub cmd2_Click()

If counter = 0 And cardTwoPickedColor < 10 Then
color = cardTwoPickedColor

Select Case cardTwoPickedColor
Case 0
picture2.Picture = LoadPicture("C:\vb\red.bmp")
x = "RED"
Case 1
picture2.Picture = LoadPicture("C:\vb\green.bmp")
x = "GREEN"
Case 2
picture2.Picture = LoadPicture("C:\vb\blue.bmp")
x = "BLUE"
Case 3
picture2.Picture = LoadPicture("C:\vb\yellow.bmp")
x = "YELLOW"
End Select

Label2 = "Looking for " & x
cmd2.Caption = "Picked"
counter = counter + 1

Else
```

```
WindowsMediaPlayer1.URL = "C:\vb\chimes.wav"
cmd2.Caption = "Picked"
If color = cardTwoPickedColor Then
Select Case cardTwoPickedColor
Case 0
picture2.Picture = LoadPicture("C:\vb\red.bmp")
Case 1
picture2.Picture = LoadPicture("C:\vb\green.bmp")
Case 2
picture2.Picture = LoadPicture("C:\vb\blue.bmp")
Case 3
picture2.Picture = LoadPicture("C:\vb\yellow.bmp")
End Select

matches = matches + 1
Text1 = "Points = " & Str(matches)
totalPoints = roundPoints + matches
Text2 = "Total Points = " & Str(totalPoints)
Label1 = "Winner"
counter = 0

Else: WindowsMediaPlayer1.URL = "C:\vb\chord.wav"
Select Case cardTwoPickedColor
Case 0
picture2.Picture = LoadPicture("C:\vb\red.bmp")
Case 1
picture2.Picture = LoadPicture("C:\vb\green.bmp")
Case 2
picture2.Picture = LoadPicture("C:\vb\blue.bmp")
Case 3
picture2.Picture = LoadPicture("C:\vb\yellow.bmp")
End Select
End If
End If
cardTwoPickedColor = 11
End Sub
```

```
Private Sub cmd3_Click()

If counter = 0 And cardThreePickedColor < 10 Then
color = cardThreePickedColor

Select Case cardThreePickedColor
Case 0
picture3.Picture = LoadPicture("C:\vb\red.bmp")
x = "RED"
Case 1
picture3.Picture = LoadPicture("C:\vb\green.bmp")
x = "GREEN"
Case 2
picture3.Picture = LoadPicture("C:\vb\blue.bmp")
x = "BLUE"
Case 3
picture3.Picture = LoadPicture("C:\vb\yellow.bmp")
x = "yellow"
End Select

Label1 = "Looking for " & x
cmd3.Caption = "Picked"
counter = counter + 1

Else
WindowsMediaPlayer1.URL = "C:\vb\chimes.wav"
cmd3.Caption = "Picked"

If cardThreePickedColor = color Then
Select Case cardThreePickedColor
Case 0
picture3.Picture = LoadPicture("C:\vb\red.bmp")
Case 1
picture3.Picture = LoadPicture("C:\vb\green.bmp")
Case 2
picture3.Picture = LoadPicture("C:\vb\blue.bmp")
Case 3
```

```vb
picture3.Picture = LoadPicture("C:\vb\yellow.bmp")
End Select

matches = matches + 1
Text1 = "Points = " & Str(matches)
totalPoints = roundPoints + matches
Text2 = "Total Points = " & Str(totalPoints)
Label1 = "That's It !"
counter = 0

Else: WindowsMediaPlayer1.URL = "C:\vb\chord.wav"

Select Case cardThreePickedColor
Case 0
picture3.Picture = LoadPicture("C:\vb\red.bmp")
Case 1
picture3.Picture = LoadPicture("C:\vb\green.bmp")
Case 2
picture3.Picture = LoadPicture("C:\vb\blue.bmp")
Case 3
picture3.Picture = LoadPicture("C:\vb\Yellow.bmp")
End Select
End If
End If
cardThreePickedColor = 12
End Sub
```

```vb
Private Sub cmd4_Click()

If counter = 0 And cardFourPickedColor < 10 Then
color = cardFourPickedColor

Select Case cardFourPickedColor
Case 0
picture4.Picture = LoadPicture("C:\vb\red.bmp")
x = "RED"
Case 1
```

```
picture4.Picture = LoadPicture("C:\vb\green.bmp")
x = "GREEN"
Case 2
picture4.Picture = LoadPicture("C:\vb\blue.bmp")
x = "BLUE"
Case 3
picture4.Picture = LoadPicture("C:\vb\Yellow.bmp")
x = "yellow"
End Select

Label1 = "Looking for " & x
cmd4.Caption = "Picked"
counter = counter + 1

Else
WindowsMediaPlayer1.URL = "C:\vb\chimes.wav"
cmd4.Caption = "Picked"
If cardFourPickedColor = color Then

Select Case cardFourPickedColor
Case 0
picture4.Picture = LoadPicture("C:\vb\red.bmp")
Case 1
picture4.Picture = LoadPicture("C:\vb\green.bmp")
Case 2
picture4.Picture = LoadPicture("C:\vb\blue.bmp")
Case 3
picture4.Picture = LoadPicture("C:\vb\Yellow.bmp")
End Select

matches = matches + 1
Text1 = "Points = " & Str(matches)
totalPoints = roundPoints + matches
Text2 = "Total Points = " & Str(totalPoints)
Label1 = "You Win"
counter = 0
```

```vb
Else: WindowsMediaPlayer1.URL = "C:\vb\chord.wav"

Select Case cardFourPickedColor
Case 0
picture4.Picture = LoadPicture("C:\vb\red.bmp")
Case 1
picture4.Picture = LoadPicture("C:\vb\green.bmp")
Case 2
picture4.Picture = LoadPicture("C:\vb\blue.bmp")
Case 3
picture4.Picture = LoadPicture("C:\vb\yellow.bmp")
End Select
End If
End If
cardFourPickedColor = 13
End Sub
```

```vb
Private Sub cmd5_Click()

If counter = 0 And cardFivePickedColor < 10 Then
color = cardFivePickedColor
Select Case cardFivePickedColor
Case 0
picture5.Picture = LoadPicture("C:\vb\red.bmp")
x = "RED"
Case 1
picture5.Picture = LoadPicture("C:\vb\green.bmp")
x = "GREEN"
Case 2
picture5.Picture = LoadPicture("C:\vb\blue.bmp")
x = "BLUE"
Case 3
picture5.Picture = LoadPicture("C:\vb\yellow.bmp")
x = "Yellow"
End Select

Label1 = "Looking for " & x
```

```
cmd5.Caption = "Picked"
counter = counter + 1


Else
WindowsMediaPlayer1.URL = "C:\vb\chimes.wav"
cmd5.Caption = "Picked"
If cardFivePickedColor = color Then
Select Case cardFivePickedColor
Case 0
picture5.Picture = LoadPicture("C:\vb\red.bmp")
Case 1
picture5.Picture = LoadPicture("C:\vb\green.bmp")
Case 2
picture5.Picture = LoadPicture("C:\vb\blue.bmp")
Case 3
picture5.Picture = LoadPicture("C:\vb\yellow.bmp")
End Select


matches = matches + 1
Text1 = "Points = " & Str(matches)
totalPoints = roundPoints + matches
Text2 = "Total Points = " & Str(totalPoints)
Label1 = "Another Point !"
counter = 0


Else: WindowsMediaPlayer1.URL = "C:\vb\chord.wav"


Select Case cardFivePickedColor
Case 0
picture5.Picture = LoadPicture("C:\vb\red.bmp")
Case 1
picture5.Picture = LoadPicture("C:\vb\green.bmp")
Case 2
picture5.Picture = LoadPicture("C:\vb\blue.bmp")
Case 3
picture5.Picture = LoadPicture("C:\vb\yellow.bmp")
End Select
```

```vb
End If
End If
cardFivePickedColor = 14
End Sub
```

```vb
Private Sub cmd6_Click()

If counter = 0 And cardSixPickedColor < 10 Then
color = cardSixPickedColor

Select Case cardSixPickedColor
Case 0
picture6.Picture = LoadPicture("C:\vb\red.bmp")
x = "RED"
Case 1
picture6.Picture = LoadPicture("C:\vb\green.bmp")
x = "GREEN"
Case 2
picture6.Picture = LoadPicture("C:\vb\blue.bmp")
x = "BLUE"
Case 3
picture6.Picture = LoadPicture("C:\vb\yellow.bmp")
x = "Yellow"
End Select

Label1 = "Looking for " & x
cmd6.Caption = "Picked"
counter = counter + 1

Else
WindowsMediaPlayer1.URL = "C:\vb\chimes.wav"
cmd6.Caption = "Picked"
If cardSixPickedColor = color Then
Select Case cardSixPickedColor
Case 0
picture6.Picture = LoadPicture("C:\vb\red.bmp")
Case 1
```

```
picture6.Picture = LoadPicture("C:\vb\green.bmp")
Case 2
picture6.Picture = LoadPicture("C:\vb\blue.bmp")
Case 3
picture6.Picture = LoadPicture("C:\vb\yellow.bmp")
End Select

matches = matches + 1
Text1 = "Points = " & Str(matches)
totalPoints = roundPoints + matches
Text2 = "Total Points = " & Str(totalPoints)
Label1 = "Good Pick"
counter = 0

Else: WindowsMediaPlayer1.URL = "C:\vb\chord.wav"

Select Case cardSixPickedColor
Case 0
picture6.Picture = LoadPicture("C:\vb\red.bmp")
Case 1
picture6.Picture = LoadPicture("C:\vb\green.bmp")
Case 2
picture6.Picture = LoadPicture("C:\vb\blue.bmp")
Case 3
picture6.Picture = LoadPicture("C:\vb\yellow.bmp")
End Select
End If
End If
cardSixPickedColor = 15
End Sub
```

```
Private Sub cmd7_Click()

If counter = 0 And cardSevenPickedColor < 10 Then
color = cardSevenPickedColor

Select Case cardSevenPickedColor
```

```
Case 0
picture7.Picture = LoadPicture("C:\vb\red.bmp")
x = "RED"
Case 1
picture7.Picture = LoadPicture("C:\vb\green.bmp")
x = "GREEN"
Case 2
picture7.Picture = LoadPicture("C:\vb\blue.bmp")
x = "BLUE"
Case 3
picture7.Picture = LoadPicture("C:\vb\yellow.bmp")
x = "YELLOW"
End Select

Label1 = "Looking for " & x
cmd7.Caption = "Picked"
counter = counter + 1

Else
WindowsMediaPlayer1.URL = "C:\vb\chimes.wav"
cmd7.Caption = "Picked"
If cardSevenPickedColor = color Then
Select Case cardSevenPickedColor
Case 0
picture7.Picture = LoadPicture("C:\vb\red.bmp")
Case 1
picture7.Picture = LoadPicture("C:\vb\green.bmp")
Case 2
picture7.Picture = LoadPicture("C:\vb\blue.bmp")
Case 3
picture7.Picture = LoadPicture("C:\vb\yellow.bmp")
End Select

matches = matches + 1
Text1 = "Points = " & Str(matches)
totalPoints = roundPoints + matches
Text2 = "Total Points = " & Str(totalPoints)
```

```
Label1 = "Great Job !"
counter = 0

Else: WindowsMediaPlayer1.URL = "C:\vb\chord.wav"

Select Case cardSevenPickedColor
Case 0
picture7.Picture = LoadPicture("C:\vb\red.bmp")
Case 1
picture7.Picture = LoadPicture("C:\vb\green.bmp")
Case 2
picture7.Picture = LoadPicture("C:\vb\blue.bmp")
Case 3
picture7.Picture = LoadPicture("C:\vb\yellow.bmp")
End Select
End If
End If
cardSevenPickedColor = 16
End Sub
```

```
Private Sub cmd8_Click()

If counter = 0 And cardEightPickedColor < 10 Then
color = cardEightPickedColor

Select Case cardEightPickedColor
Case 0
picture8.Picture = LoadPicture("C:\vb\red.bmp")
x = "RED"
Case 1
picture8.Picture = LoadPicture("C:\vb\green.bmp")
x = "GREEN"
Case 2
picture8.Picture = LoadPicture("C:\vb\blue.bmp")
x = "BLUE"
Case 3
picture8.Picture = LoadPicture("C:\vb\yellow.bmp")
```

```
        x = "YELLOW"
      End Select

      Label1 = "Looking for " & x
      cmd8.Caption = "Picked"
      counter = counter + 1

      Else
      WindowsMediaPlayer1.URL = "C:\vb\chimes.wav"
      cmd8.Caption = "Picked"
      If cardEightPickedColor = color Then

      Select Case cardEightPickedColor
      Case 0
      picture8.Picture = LoadPicture("C:\vb\red.bmp")
      Case 1
      picture8.Picture = LoadPicture("C:\vb\green.bmp")
      Case 2
      picture8.Picture = LoadPicture("C:\vb\blue.bmp")
      Case 3
      picture8.Picture = LoadPicture("C:\vb\yellow.bmp")
      End Select

      matches = matches + 1
      Text1 = "Points = " & Str(matches)
      totalPoints = roundPoints + matches
      Text2 = "Total Points = " & Str(totalPoints)
      Label1 = "Win !"
      counter = 0

      Else: WindowsMediaPlayer1.URL = "C:\vb\chord.wav"
      Select Case cardEightPickedColor
      Case 0
      picture8.Picture = LoadPicture("C:\vb\red.bmp")
      Case 1
      picture8.Picture = LoadPicture("C:\vb\green.bmp")
      Case 2
```

```
picture8.Picture = LoadPicture("C:\vb\blue.bmp")
Case 3
picture8.Picture = LoadPicture("C:\vb\yellow.bmp")
End Select
End If
End If
cardEightPickedColor = 17
End Sub


'hide colors and zero counter
Private Sub cmdReset_Click()
picture1.Picture = LoadPicture("C:\vb\black.bmp")
picture2.Picture = LoadPicture("C:\vb\black.bmp")
picture3.Picture = LoadPicture("C:\vb\black.bmp")
picture4.Picture = LoadPicture("C:\vb\black.bmp")
picture5.Picture = LoadPicture("C:\vb\black.bmp")
picture6.Picture = LoadPicture("C:\vb\black.bmp")
picture7.Picture = LoadPicture("C:\vb\black.bmp")
picture8.Picture = LoadPicture("C:\vb\black.bmp")
GameCounter = 0
matches = 0
totalPoints = 0
roundPoints = 0
totalMatches = 0
Label1 = "New Game"
Text1 = "Press Memorize"
Text2 = "Start New Game"
End Sub


Private Sub cmdExit_Click()
End
End Sub
```

Code Listing 10.2 Memory game

The code length is quite long due to much redundancy necessary for the eight images and associated command buttons. The code can be copied and pasted with minor variations for each specific control. Towards the beginning of the memorize section, variables are reset for the new round, and the command button caption properties are reset to their appropriate number since later in the code, their caption changes to the word *picked*. Each of the buttons should also be captioned with their numbers in the property box so that they will appear at the game's start-up. A very large *do-while loop* is used in the *memorize* section to select a random pattern of images, where four pairs of different color images are chosen to appear for play. The loop starting and stopping points are noted with comments in the code. The colors are arbitrarily assigned as 0. red 1. green, 2. blue, and 3. yellow. The random numbers zero through 3 are assigned to the variables *cardOne* through *cardEight,* representing the location of the card. Once two colors are assigned to card locations, then the process is locked out using the variable cardOneSelect through cardEightSelect. This is done by using multiple AND conditional statements. (Remember, the variable count starts at zero and includes zero.) The color numbers are assigned to variables pic1 through pic8, and upon exit of the color selection loop, select case conditional code populates each card location using the path to load the correct pictures.

The play command button hides the cards after the game's player has memorized them by loading a black picture into each image location on the form. The button also displays the number of correct color matches for the round in the left side text box named Text1.

The reset button will zero the game counter variable, which stops play after 10 rounds. It is incremented each time the memorize button is clicked. Reset code also sets variables to zero to start a new set of rounds and displays black pictures in the image boxes so that the user can restart the game from scratch. Restart messages are also loaded into the text boxes and the label.

The numbered command buttons are utilized during the game to match the colors. Once they are picked, a lockout occurs by setting the numbered command button variables cardOnePickedColor through cardEightPickedColor above 10, so they cannot meet the conditional statements. A select case condition is used to display what the following color needs to be for a match. The information appears at the bottom of the form in Lable1. This player information is a bit redundant, and you may wish to eliminate it from the program to clean up the code. A counter variable is used to determine when the button is being clicked, as the second part of the match process. Chimes are sounded, and Winning messages are generated if the color is a match; otherwise, the chord.wav sounds and a loss is noted in the player feedback.

This game is highly adaptable, and the colors could be replaced with pictures associated with names and sounds for use as an early learning program for children. The form could also be expanded to full screen to add more elements. This project shows excellent use of random numbers in a constructive game.

Chapter Ten Summary

We expanded on using random numbers and had some fun creating a game of chance and an educational game for children and older people with cognitive challenges. We found that code can often be quite repetitive in producing games or other programs that feature many rules or options. It is quite a messy looking job at first glance, but on closer examination, it can be seen that much of the work is copying and pasting sections of code while only making minor changes. Again, we saw the form layout, and using the properties window is an excellent help in the overall construction of a program, as is the naming of controls and variables to be somewhat descriptive of their purpose. It should also be noted how vital documentation during the coding process is in helping others understand your intentions and program flow. It will also help you if the code is to be modified by you at a later date, since it most probably would be tough to recall the logical thought process you were using the first time. Also, there are many different ways to code a program. The most straightforward approach using the least amount of code lines seems to be best, but if the program works, in my opinion, the coding is correct.

Chapter Eleven

Unfinished Business

Section 11.1. The One-button Bandit Game

The last game presented to you is a work in progress. We are offering a skeleton program that can you can build on in any number of directions. A popular attraction in casinos is the one-armed bandit slot machine. Our project can be further developed in that way, or modified as a learning tool, as was our last program. This project will use pictures rather than solid colors and require the picture size and image on the form to be similar in size. The number of photos may vary. We are using three, as shown in Figure 11.1.

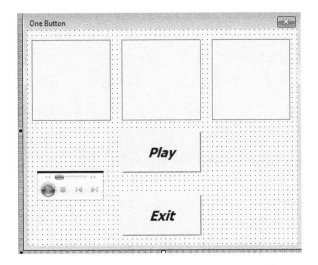

Figure 11.1 One button game

Although it is best to rename objects on a form, since the form is so fundamental, I am using the default names and using the caption window to display the word *Play* in bold 16 point font. We are using the Windows Media Player again in the nonvisible mode with its visible property set to false in the property window. Even on a small project, the code can be somewhat repetitive, as shown in Code Listing 11.1.

```
'one button game
Dim first, second, third As Integer

Private Sub CommandButton1_Click()
Randomize
first = Int((3 * Rnd) + 1)
second = Int((3 * Rnd) + 1)
third = Int((3 * Rnd) + 1)

Select Case first
Case 1
Image1.Picture = LoadPicture("C:\vb\apple.bmp")
Case 2
Image1.Picture = LoadPicture("C:\vb\banana.bmp")
Case 3
Image1.Picture = LoadPicture("C:\vb\cherry.bmp")
End Select

Select Case second
Case 1
Image2.Picture = LoadPicture("C:\vb\apple.bmp")
Case 2
Image2.Picture = LoadPicture("C:\vb\banana.bmp")
Case 3
Image2.Picture = LoadPicture("C:\vb\cherry.bmp")
End Select

Select Case third
Case 1
Image3.Picture = LoadPicture("C:\vb\apple.bmp")
Case 2
Image3.Picture = LoadPicture("C:\vb\banana.bmp")
```

```
Case 3
Image3.Picture = LoadPicture("C:\vb\cherry.bmp")
End Select

If first = second And first = third Then
WindowsMediaPlayer1.URL = "C:\vb\chimes.wav"
MsgBox "Winner"
End If
End Sub
_____

Private Sub cmdExit_Click()
End
End Sub
```

Code Listing 11.1 One button game

In the general declaration section, the variables *first*, *second*, and *third* are listed on one line separated by commas, which is the alternative to listing each on separate lines. After we generate three random numbers for the variables, they are used to select pictures using the select case procedure. *If/then else/if* statements could also be used, but the Select Case procedure is a little cleaner. The Windows Media Player sounds the chimes, and a winning message box pops up if there is a match of all three pictures.

We are leaving this basic game as a project to build on. You may wish to add a score counter, place bets, and possibly determine a total, or even have a Loan Shark assist in funding a losing player. On the other hand, you might change the pictures to animals, use the media player to play animal sounds, or use labels to show spelling as a learning tool for young children. We leave this as a final project for you to complete.

Section 11.2. Wrap-up.

Programming, like any skill, is learned by doing. It is a process of using computer commands to generate results. Most of the time, programs will not function correctly at first and must be debugged. Usually, misspellings or coding language issues lead to what is termed a syntax error. Painstakingly close examination of the typing of each word, character, and punctuation mark may solve the problem. Sometimes a trial and error process will solve the problem too. VBA, just like VB, allows a programmer to set break-points in a program to stop during the execution phase and then be stepped line by line through the problematic area while checking progress along the way as variables change. A more insidious problem has the term *logic error*. That is when an incorrect thought process may have been used in finding the solution, and a rethink may be necessary for the overall scheme in obtaining a correct result. Thankfully we humans are pretty good at solving problems, and the vast majority of issues we encounter with any programming language relate in some way to syntax errors.

Visual Basic is a powerful programming language that professional programmers somewhat dislike, most probably because of its ease of use. There may be some issues with the language, but in general, it is an entertaining, useful, and productive tool incorporated into the Microsoft Office Suite. Our goal was to introduce you to it, and show just how, with a little work and practice, anyone can do computer programming. I'm not a software expert, but I have fun with it and hope you found some of the projects enjoyable. I encourage you to modify the projects in this book and to look deeper into the subject. Whether it is VBA, or another language that interests you, good luck, practice, and when necessary, hack. (Hack meaning to try things to see if they work.)